A Whole-School Behaviour Policy

A Practical Guide

ROY LUND

KOGAN
PAGE

First published in 1996

Apart from any fair dealing for the purposes of research or private study, or criticism or review, as permitted under the Copyright, Designs and Patents Act 1988, this publication may only be reproduced, stored or transmitted, in any form or by any means, with the prior permission in writing of the publishers, or in the case of reprographic reproduction in accordance with the terms of licences issued by the Copyright Licensing Agency. Enquiries concerning reproduction outside those terms should be sent to the publishers at the undermentioned address:

Kogan Page Limited
120 Pentonville Road
London N1 9JN

© Roy Lund, 1996

While the author and the publisher have made every effort to ensure the accuracy and appropriateness of the advice given in this book, no responsibility is accepted for any consequences of this advice being followed.

British Library Cataloguing in Publication Data

A CIP record for this book is available from the British Library.

ISBN 0 7494 2058 8

Typeset by Kogan Page
Printed and bound in Great Britain by Biddles Ltd, Guildford and King's Lynn

Contents

Acknowledgements

I would like to thank Sue Panter for her help in reviewing the final draft of this book and for making several suggestions for improvement, some of which have been adopted.

I would also like to thank Jenny Lund for her help over child protection issues and for help with the final editing.

Any mistakes and omissions that remain are entirely mine.

I am grateful to HMSO and to SCAA for permission to quote from their publications. Crown copyright is reproduced with the permission of the Controller of HMSO.

Roy Lund,
September 1996

What this book is about and how to use it

This book provides schools with a practical framework for reviewing, developing and implementing a whole-school behaviour policy – in less time than if the school had started from scratch. At the same time, the resulting policy should be in full accordance with the ethos of the establishment and the school development plan, and compatible with the OFSTED inspection evaluation criteria. It can be used by secondary, primary, upper, middle, first, nursery and special schools and Pupil Referral Units (PRUs). It will also be useful to those working in children's homes and centres and other residential provision for children.

As this book is intended for a wide readership, some of the suggestions and procedures will not necessarily apply to every institution. Readers should take what they want out of it and ignore the rest.

Schools want to know what to do when they have problems over behaviour; who should do it, how it should be done and when it should be done. They also want to anticipate any snags they are likely to meet and prepare strategies for dealing with them if they do arise. They do not want reams of academic research. The materials in this book are designed to provide common-sense advice in a practical framework. At the same time, reference has been made to useful sources, which can be followed up if the reader has a particular interest or concern.

Current concerns about behaviour in schools

Teachers, political leaders and the public have never been more concerned about the behaviour of children in schools. There are almost daily newspaper reports of assaults against teachers and demands for action.

At the same time, schools are worried about the effect of inappropriate behaviour on standards. Schools are conscious that any disruptive behaviour can affect teaching and learning, and are worried about its effects on inspection reports. The simplest and most effective way of removing such behaviour from a school is to exclude the offending pupils.

In 1992, the National Union of Teachers (NUT) commissioned a report from the consultants Coopers and Lybrand based on returns from 26 of the 117 local authorities in England and Wales. They found that exclusions had risen by one-fifth to 25,000 in the previous year. Ashworth, of the Advisory Centre for Education, and Smith, of the National Children's Bureau, are reported as saying that schools wanted to improve their images (Pyke, 1992).

The Association of Metropolitan Authorities' survey into special educational needs has gathered evidence that schools are becoming less tolerant of pupils with behavioural problems (AMA, 1995). Schools are excluding younger children and more statements are being completed for children with emotional and behavioural difficulties (HMSO, 1993). At the same time, increased numbers of children with statements of special educational needs are being removed from mainstream schools to separate special schooling. In February 1996, there were nearly 300 PRUs, catering for pupils who, for whatever reason, were not coping with mainstream schooling. In addition, there were approximately 220 maintained and non-maintained and approximately 40 independent Department for Education and Employment (DfEE) approved special schools for children with emotional and behavioural difficulties (EBD) throughout the country.

Stirling studied the effect of the Education Reform Act on children with emotional and behavioural difficulties in two local authorities, one a shire county and one a metropolitan borough. In both, the numbers of exclusions were rising.

> Schools reported that EBD pupils in large classes made it harder to carry out standard assessment tasks. Heads were concerned that the need to publish test scores would force schools to favour academically able pupils. Difficult and disturbed pupils, they argued, could interfere with the academic progress of other children and discourage academically able pupils from applying. A school's reputation under LMS has direct financial consequences.
>
> (Stirling, 1992)

She discusses the problems of providing statements of special educational needs, arguing that they are costly and time-consuming. There is therefore, a reluctance on the part of authorities to formally assess ('statement') children with emotional and behavioural difficulties. Exclusion, however, is both immediately available and under the school's control.

Pyke (1993) reports on research done by the MORI organization for the BBC television programme Panorama which showed that between 1990 and 1992, 66,000 pupils were excluded from schools, marking a 50 per cent increase over the two years. He quotes the OFSTED report, *Education for Disaffected Pupils* (1993) which referred to one authority where the number of permanent exclusions rose from 99 to 149 between 1989 and 1991. The OFSTED inspectors suggest these reasons for increased exclusions:

- increased stress in the family
- reduced teacher tolerance
- a view of exclusion as a natural part of the punishment procedures
- an attempt to be seen as tough on discipline
- a response to poor attendance rates
- a result of staffing difficulties
- a decline in the number of informal arrangements between headteachers; and
- an attempt to secure additional support or a different placement for SEN pupils. (Pyke, 1993)

The *Code of Practice on the Identification and Assessment of Special Educational Needs* (DfE, 1994b) gives a statutory requirement for a stage-by-stage process for identifying and assessing the needs of pupils with emotional and behavioural difficulties. In practice, this process is time-consuming and complicated. While it is going on, disaffection sets in for pupil and teacher; behaviour deteriorates and tolerance diminishes, leading to exclusion. Further discussion of the needs of pupils with emotional and behavioural difficulties may be found in Chapter 9, The difficult pupil.

Why develop a whole-school behaviour policy?

Schools are complicated institutions. Unless the members of the school community behave appropriately towards each other, the community cannot function. Below are some of the reasons for establishing a whole-school behaviour policy. (*Note* that the order of priority might well be different for different schools: you will need to develop your own, specific criteria.)

- To provide an opportunity to put shared values about the ways school communities should behave into practice.

- To develop a positive reputation for the school within the community.

- To enable all members of the school community to behave appropriately towards each other and to cooperate in teaching and learning.

- To provide a positive school ethos, conducive to teaching and learning.

- To enable the development of high self-esteem in all members of the school community.

- To enable each pupil to have an appropriate environment for learning and each teacher to have a suitable environment for teaching.

- To define what is meant by appropriate behaviour and inappropriate behaviour.

- To enable appropriate rewards, sanctions and punishments to be developed.

- To enable the school's system of rewards, sanctions and punishments to be accepted as fair and reasonable by the whole school community.

- To provide each teacher with an appropriate range of strategies for the most difficult pupils.

- To clarify roles over behaviour management.

The rationale behind the approach used in this book

The rationale behind the materials in this book is that if all members of a school community have values and beliefs which demonstrate respect and consideration for each individual, and if there are accepted, shared procedures for the way in which all members of the school community behave towards each other, then there will be very few children who need extra help and support. There is also an underlying assumption that children who are motivated to learn do not generally behave unacceptably.

The basic principles

1. That schools do indeed make a difference to behaviour. This point is discussed further in Chapter 1, School ethos and effectiveness.

2. That all members of the school community should be involved in and have ownership of any school behaviour policy. It needs to be a *whole-school* policy.

3. All members of the school community should have shared positive values about the way in which individuals should behave and be treated.

4. There should be strategies for changing any negative attitudes about the behaviour of all members of the school community into positive attitudes.

5. There should be procedures for rewarding and celebrating achievement in learning and behaviour and for dealing with inappropriate behaviour in a positive manner, which are understood, accepted and practised by the whole school community.

6. If these conditions are met, *there will be very few children who need additional special help*. If the policies and procedures are right in every classroom and around the school, almost all children behave appropriately for almost all of the time. For this reason, Chapter 9, The difficult pupil, is at the end of the first part of this book. Dealing with the individual behaviour of the child whose behaviour does not seem to respond to any approach is a last consideration, not a first.

OFSTED evaluation criteria on behaviour

As well as the materials in this book, schools will want to pay attention to the criteria which are used by OFSTED in their inspections.

There are three OFSTED handbooks relating to the inspection of schools: *Guidance on the Inspection of Nursery and Primary Schools* (OFSTED, 1995a), *Guidance on the Inspection of Secondary Schools* (OFSTED, 1995b) and *Guidance on the Inspection of Special Schools* (OFSTED, 1995c). In addition, there is an overall *Framework for the Inspections of Schools* (OFSTED, 1995d).

Behaviour is crucially linked to motivation, achievement and hence to standards. This is recognized by OFSTED in their inspections under Section 9 of the Education (Schools) Act 1992 (HMSO, 1992). In the *Framework for the Inspection of Schools*, schools are judged as to the 'educational standards achieved by pupils at the school' and the 'quality of education provided'. Inspectors use observation forms to record evidence of standards in:

Teaching
Response
Attainment, and
Progress.

In all these areas, observations of the behaviour of the pupils and the way it is managed, is an important part of the evidence recorded on the observation form, especially that relating to response.

There are also three main inspection aspects which specifically refer to behaviour:

4.2 Attitudes, behaviour and personal development,
5.3 Pupils' spiritual, moral, social and cultural development, and
5.4 Support, guidance and pupils' welfare.

The following extracts show how behaviour issues are inspected by OFSTED:

4.2 Attitudes, behaviour and personal development

Inspectors must evaluate and report on pupils' response to the teaching and other provision made by the school, highlighting strengths and weaknesses, as shown by:

- their attitudes to learning;
- their behaviour, including incidence of exclusions;
- the quality of relationships in the school including the degree of racial harmony, where applicable;
- other aspects of their personal development, including their contributions to the life of the community.

Judgements should be based on the extent to which pupils:

◆ show interest in their work and are able to sustain concentration and develop their capacity for personal study;
◆ behave well in and around the school, and are courteous and trustworthy and show respect for property;
◆ form constructive relationships with one another, with teachers and other adults, and work collaboratively when required;
◆ show respect for other people's feelings, values and beliefs;
◆ show initiative and are willing to take responsibility.

(Framework, OFSTED, 1995d, p.17)

Under 'Inspection focus' for 4.2, the handbooks state (among other factors):

■ In nursery and primary schools, and PRUs, good communication with parents is the basis for productive attitudes to learning, good behaviour and personal development.... Good behaviour is vital to productive learning, the quality of life in the school and to the functioning of the school as an orderly community.   (Nursery and Primary Schools, OFSTED, 1995a, p.61)

■ Pupils' attitudes have a significant bearing on their attainment and progress and can be strongly influenced by what schools do. Good behaviour is vital to productive learning, and the quality of life in the school and to the functioning of the school as an orderly community.

(Secondary Schools, OFSTED, 1995b, p.61)

■ Good communication with parents is the basis for productive attitudes to learning, good behaviour and positive personal development. Pupils' attitudes have a significant bearing on their attainment and progress and can be strongly influenced by what schools do.

(Special Schools, OFSTED, 1995c, p.61)

■ On the basis of the team's observations in lessons and around the school, inspectors should judge pupils' behaviour and its effect on their learning and on the school.

(Nursery Schools, OFSTED, 1995a, p.61; Secondary Schools, OFSTED, 1995b, p.61; Special Schools, OFSTED, 1995c, p.61)

■ Pupils in PRUs have usually experienced significant difficulties in behaviour and motivation before entering the unit. Inspectors should look for the development, from a low baseline, of positive attitudes to learning, good behaviour and personal responsibility.

(Nursery and Primary Schools, OFSTED, 1995a, p.61; Secondary Schools, OFSTED, 1995b, p.61)

■ Some pupils with special educational needs have experienced significant difficulties in behaviour and motivation before entering the school. Inspectors should look for the development, from a low baseline, of positive attitudes to learning, good behaviour and personal responsibility.

(Special Schools, OFSTED, 1995c, p.61)

5.3 Pupils' spiritual, moral, social and cultural development

Inspectors must evaluate and report on:

- The strengths and weaknesses of the school's provision for the spiritual, moral, social and cultural development of the pupils, through the curriculum and life of the school, the example set for the pupils by adults in the school; and the act of collective worship.

Judgements should be based on the extent to which the school [among other factors]:

- ◆ teaches the principles which distinguish right from wrong;
- ◆ encourages pupils to relate positively to others, take responsibility, participate fully in the community, and develop an understanding of citizenship;
(Framework, OFSTED, 1995d, p.19)

Under 'Inspection focus' for 5.3, the handbooks state (among other factors):

Overall judgements are concerned with the opportunities given for pupils to learn about and explore different values, beliefs and views and to develop and express their own. Judgements should be based on evidence from the whole curriculum and the day-to-day life of the school, including the examples set by adults and the quality of collective worship.
(Nursery and Primary Schools, OFSTED, 1995a, p.83; Secondary Schools, OFSTED, 1995b, p.89; Special Schools, OFSTED, 1995c, p.89)

Under 'Using the criteria' for 5.3, the handbooks include, among others:

Does the school teach the principles which separate right from wrong?

- The essence of moral behaviour is to build a framework of values which regulate personal behaviour through principles rather than through fear of punishment or reward. With support, nursery pupils are aware of what is acceptable and unacceptable behaviour. Older pupils are able to make moral decisions through the application of reason, even though they may not cope quite so securely with problems in which they are emotionally involved: in other words, their learning about moral issues may be at a different point from their behaviour. Moral and social education are closely related and depend on the school fostering values such as honesty, fairness and respect for truth and justice.
(Nursery and Primary Schools, OFSTED, 1995a, p.84)

- The essence of moral behaviour is to build a framework of values which regulate personal behaviour through principles rather than through fear of punishment or reward. Pupils are able to make moral decisions through the application of reason, even though they may not cope quite so securely with problems in which they are emotionally involved: in other words, their learning about moral issues may be at a different point from their behaviour. Moral and social education are closely related and depend on the school fostering values such as honesty, fairness and respect for truth and justice.
(Secondary Schools, OFSTED, 1995b, p.90; Special Schools, OFSTED, 1995c, p.90)

Does the school encourage pupils to relate effectively to others, take responsibility, participate fully in the community and develop an understanding of citizenship? [among other factors]:

- Social development hinges on an acceptance of group rules and the ability to set oneself in a wider context. For young children and those in PRUs, learning how to relate to others and take responsibility for their own actions is an important part of their education. The quality of relationships in schools is of crucial importance in forming the pupils' attitudes to good social behaviour and self-discipline.

  (Nursery and Primary Schools, OFSTED, 1995a, p.84)

- Social development hinges on an acceptance of group rules and the ability to set oneself in a wider context. Adolescents may find that the need to be socially compliant is sometimes at odds with their developing moral sensibility. Partly for this reason, the quality of relationships in schools is of crucial importance in forming pupils' attitudes to good social behaviour and self-discipline.

  (Secondary Schools, OFSTED, 1995b, p.90)

- Social development hinges on an acceptance of group rules and the ability to set oneself in a wider context. Young children and adolescents may find that the need to be socially compliant is sometimes at odds with their developing moral sensibility. Partly for this reason, the quality of relationships in schools is of crucial importance in forming pupils' attitudes to co-operation, good social behaviour and self-discipline; for many children in special schools this social development is a central aim of their education.

  (Special Schools, OFSTED, 1995c, p.90)

5.4 Support, guidance and pupils' welfare

Inspectors must evaluate and report on:

- strengths and weaknesses in the school's provision for the educational and personal support and guidance of pupils and its contribution to educational standards achieved, taking account of educational needs, and the steps taken to ensure pupils' welfare;
- the school's arrangements for child protection; and
- any matters which, in the view of inspectors, constitute a threat to health and safety.

Judgements should be based on the extent to which the school:

- ◆ provides effective support and advice for all its pupils, informed by monitoring of their academic progress, personal development, behaviour and attendance;
- ◆ has effective measures to promote discipline and good behaviour and eliminate oppressive behaviour, including all forms of harassment and bullying;
- ◆ has effective child protection policies; and
- ◆ is successful in promoting the health, safety and general well-being of its pupils.

  (Framework, OFSTED, 1995d, p.20)

Under 'Using the criteria' for 5.3, the handbooks state:

Does the school provide effective support, advice and guidance for all its pupils, informed by monitoring of their academic progress, personal development, behaviour and attendance? [among other factors]:

- Inspectors should assess how well staff interact with pupils within and outside the classroom, their accessibility and responsiveness to pupils' needs and the quality of support they give. The key is the impact on pupils' progress, general confidence and ability to cope effectively with everyday life in the school. In relation to pupils with special educational needs, particular attention should be paid to how pupils are helped to meet the objectives in their individual education plans. Inspectors need to assess the quality of liaison with support agencies and the impact on support for pupils. Where inspection priorities allow, it may be possible to discuss this with visiting staff.

Does the school have effective measures to promote discipline and good behaviour and eliminate oppressive behaviour including all forms of harassment and bullying?

- While evidence of the school's intentions can be gained from documents on policy and procedures, the emphasis should be on the consistency of practice. Evaluation against the criterion should link with Section 4.2. Attention should be given to how the school raises general awareness of behaviour issues and how it creates a climate for good behaviour, as well as how it deals with specific incidents of misbehaviour. During the inspection, observation, discussion with staff and with pupils and analysis of records will provide the basis for judgements.
  In relation to harassment and bullying, inspectors need to assess how well the school recognises and records incidents that occur, how well it deals with them and what steps are taken to prevent repetition.

Does the school have effective child protection procedures?

- Inspectors should evaluate whether the school is in a position to comply with local child protection procedures and whether the school's approach helps pupils to protect themselves and understand the importance of protecting others. A particular focus is how the school deals with instances of possible child abuse and its procedures for liaison with other agencies where children are on the child protection register. Inspectors should establish whether all staff are aware of the procedures and how they raise pupils' awareness of child protection issues.
  Where the registered inspector has reasonable grounds to believe that specific instances of possible child abuse are not being dealt with satisfactorily by the school, the relevant authority, normally the social services child protection team, should be contacted.
  (Nursery and Primary Schools, OFSTED, 1995a, p.90; Secondary Schools, OFSTED, 1995b, p.96; Special Schools, OFSTED, 1995c, p.96)

The Elton Report

Another useful source is *Discipline in Schools* (The Elton Report) (DES, 1989a) which emphasizes the importance of establishing a whole-school approach to behaviour management – one based on a positive school ethos and a set of shared values about the way in which the members of school communities should relate to each other:

> Most researchers now agree that some schools are more effective than others in promoting good work and behaviour.
> The message to heads and teachers is clear. It is that they have the power through their own efforts to improve standards of work and behaviour and the life chances of their pupils.   (DES, 1989a, paras. 3 and 4, p.88)

It is unfortunate that the report, with its wealth of useful suggestions for promoting a positive approach to behaviour management in school, was largely ignored by schools at the time of its publication in 1989. The reason was probably that schools had more than enough to contend with, following the Education Reform Act, 1988 (HMSO, 1988) and the implementation of the National Curriculum, Grant Maintained Schools, national testing and assessment of pupils, and the OFSTED framework of regular inspections. The report is still available and contains many useful, practical suggestions for schools to use in drawing up their behaviour policies.

'Pupil Behaviour and Discipline'

Circular 8/94, *Pupil Behaviour and Discipline* (DfE, 1994d) gives updated guidance and a useful framework for a whole-school behaviour policy which can be consulted alongside the materials in this book.

What should be in a whole-school behaviour policy?

Schools will vary as to what is included within the policy but there are various issues which influence the way in which members of a school community behave towards one another. In general, these can be summarized as issues relating to:

- the school, its ethos and value-system
- teaching and learning
- individual pupils, their families and cultural backgrounds.

These are explored in the first part of this book.

Some of these issues, such as child protection and bullying, are major ones which might well be dealt with as separate policies, but it is nevertheless important to ensure the compatibility of all policies concerning behaviour.

The contents of this book

The book is divided into two sections.

Section 1
The first section is designed to raise the issues that should be taken into account when drawing up the whole-school behaviour policy:

Chapter 1   School ethos and effectiveness
Chapter 2   Teaching and learning
Chapter 3   Rewards and sanctions
Chapter 4   Bullying
Chapter 5   Pupil and staff protection
Chapter 6   Equal opportunities
Chapter 7   Involving parents
Chapter 8   Support for all
Chapter 9   The difficult pupil

Section 2
The second section provides the practical framework for developing and implementing the whole-school behaviour policy based on a standard review and development model (develop; implement; review; evaluate). It opens with a flow chart (p.90) and follows the sequence:

Chapter 10   The process of developing and implementing a whole-
             school behaviour policy
Chapter 11   Establishing shared values
Chapter 12   Reviewing the operation of the current behaviour policy
Chapter 13   Developing a whole-school behaviour policy
Chapter 14   Implementing a whole-school behaviour policy

The management of the process

The success of any project is crucially linked to the effectiveness of the person who manages it. The person who manages the development of this project must be a member of the school's Senior Management Team (SMT), have the confidence of the whole community, the enthusiasm to succeed and the time to finish it. It is suggested that this person, a Key Person (KP), is appointed by the school's SMT and governors to oversee the project and that he or she should set up an Action Group (AG). In large schools, the AG should comprise a small group of teachers, support staff and governors. In small schools and PRUs, all teaching and support staff could take part, together with some of the governors. The KP would decide on the tasks for each member of the AG, including drafting the policy.

The KP and AG will consider Section 1 of the book, which is designed to raise issues that need to be taken into account in any whole-school behaviour policy. The issues have been dealt with only briefly, as adults working in schools are too busy to delve into vast amounts of literature and it has been necessary to be selective. The 'References and further reading' section at the end suggests additional background reading. It should be borne in mind that some sources will be more appropriate than others to a particular phase or a particular school.

The KP and AG will then work through Section 2 of the book (Chapters 10–14), which is designed to enable the practical review, development and implementation of a whole-school behaviour policy.

At the end of the project, the school should have a new whole-school behaviour policy in operation.

Good and bad behaviour or appropriate and inappropriate behaviour?

Adults continually tell children that their behaviour is *good* or *bad* and more specifically, that they are *good* when they behave well and *bad* when they behave badly. Effective behaviour policies separate the child from the behaviour: 'We want you – we do not want this behaviour'. This implies the acceptance of the child as a person while not accepting or condoning his or her inappropriate behaviour. In such a model, the concept of a '*good child*' or a '*bad child*' is not helpful.

So far there is the underlying assumption that inappropriate behaviour is overt. This is the behaviour which most concerns the teacher in the classroom or around the school because it is related to the management of the pupils. There are, however, other forms of inappropriate behaviour, which can demonstrate that the individual is not settled within the community. These could include non communication, quiet non-compliance, being off-task and poor concentration.

By using the terms *appropriate* and *inappropriate* for behaviour, it can be much more context-specific, ie, relate to the situation in which it actually occurs. This reinforces the notion of the importance of appropriate behaviour within a group setting and the behavioural responsibilities of each individual within the group, based on common values. It also helps target-setting for behaviour and reparation, as well as the recognition that each incident is complete in itself. Consequently, the terms *appropriate* and *inappropriate* behaviour are used throughout this book. With a little practice, children and adults in schools can get used to this more positive terminology!

Section 1

Chapter 1

School ethos and effectiveness

Schools are institutions for teaching and learning and the standards of these are increasingly being judged, not least by OFSTED (OFSTED, 1995d). Teaching and learning cannot take place if pupils in the group are behaving inappropriately. Effective teaching and learning is more likely to take place within an environment where all members of the school community understand, and work within, an effective whole-school behaviour policy based on a set of shared values and a positive ethos.

The 'effective schools' research demonstrates clearly that there are certain factors in schools which make a difference to the general ethos of the school and hence to teaching and learning; these are shown in Table 1.1.

Table 1.1 *Eleven factors for effective schools (from Sammons, et al., 1995, p. 8)*

1. Professional leadership	Firm and purposeful A participative approach The leading professional
2. Shared vision and goals	Unity of purpose Consistency of practice Collegiality and collaboration
3. A learning environment	An orderly atmosphere An attractive working environment

4. Concentration on teaching and learning	Maximisation of learning time Academic emphasis Focus on achievement
5. Purposeful teaching	Efficient organisation Clarity of purpose Structured lessons Adaptive practice
6. High expectations	High expectations all round Communicating expectations Providing intellectual challenge
7. Positive reinforcement	Clear and fair discipline Feedback
8. Monitoring progress	Monitoring pupil performance Evaluating school performance
9. Pupil rights and responsibilities	Raising pupil self-esteem Positions of responsibility Control of work
10. Home–school partnership	Parental involvement in their children's learning
11. A learning organisation	School-based staff development

The majority of school effectiveness studies have focused on teaching and learning and not on personal and social factors – the factors usually associated with behaviour and the management of behaviour. However, it will be noted all these 11 factors can be related to behaviour:

1. Professional leadership

Any behaviour policy is likely to be unsuccessful unless there is a 'Key Person' (KP) appointed by the senior management team (SMT) committed to the policy and the values which underpin it. This member of the SMT should be responsible for reviewing and evaluating the policy and for supporting staff through the process of its development and implementation.

2. Shared vision and goals

Effective policies are those which are based on shared values, consensus and ownership by the whole-school community.

3. A learning environment

Shared routines, in learning and behaviour, both in the classroom and around the school, give a sense of security to the children and teachers and encourage a stable working environment and appropriate behaviour.

4. Concentration on teaching and learning

A work-orientated environment, in which all children are encouraged to achieve in learning, promotes appropriate behaviour. Within this, each individual's unique, personal contribution is valued.

5. Purposeful teaching

Disaffection is often caused by the apparent irrelevance of what is being taught, both from the perspective of some teachers as well as from the perspective of some pupils. Inappropriate behaviour, which affects teaching and learning, rarely occurs where there is stimulating teaching, differentiated according to the learning, cultural, social and *emotional* needs of each individual child.

6. High expectations

Children need to feel that their abilities are being stretched but at the same time need to experience personal success in learning. This is more effective if they are helped to achieve their own personal targets.

7. Positive reinforcement

The system of rewards, sanctions and punishments should be seen to be fair and owned by the whole-school community. The effect of the celebration of achievement is to motivate the children to learn and to behave appropriately. (For some children, achievement must be celebrated in a way which does not give publicity.)

8. Monitoring progress

Realistic individual targets for children in learning and behaviour help to promote achievement. Targets are more effective if children and their parents/carers are involved in developing them.

9. Pupil rights and responsibilities

Children with high self-esteem tend to behave appropriately (see Chapter 2, Teaching and learning). High self-esteem can be encouraged by the setting of realistic targets for learning and behaviour for each child and by the celebration of success.

Children need to feel valued as persons.

Children have a right for their achievements to be valued and have a responsibility to value the achievements of others.

Children need to know who they can turn to with their worries and to have the confidence that they will be listened to and treated seriously.

Rules about behaviour are more likely to be accepted by the children if they are given the responsibility of helping to develop them.

10. Home–school partnership

Behaviour policies are more likely to be effective if they are understood, accepted and supported by parents/carers. Parents/carers can have an important role in setting targets for and celebrating success in, achievements in learning and behaviour.

11. A learning organization

Shared enjoyment in teaching and learning leads to appropriate behaviour. Most children who are stimulated by the teaching on offer and motivated to learn, do not behave inappropriately.

Behaviour and effective schools

Adults working in schools spend a great deal of time worrying about and attempting to control, the behaviour of a few individual children. If, however, whole-school behaviour policies are developed and introduced which are based on shared values and positive beliefs about success in teaching and learning and appropriate behaviour, then there will be very few children whose behaviour remains inappropriate (see Chapter 9, The difficult pupil).

However, behaviour *management* and discipline in general is only a small part of a school's behaviour policy. *Behaviour policies are about enabling all members of the school community to feel valued, to have their achievements valued and to behave appropriately towards each other*. This is why the starting point for the development of the whole-school behaviour policy, as outlined in Chapter 10, The process of developing and implementing a whole-school behaviour policy, is the school's shared values.

The following basic principles of what makes an effective school are highlighted in *Discipline in Schools* (DES, 1989a) and in the effective schools research:

- Policies based on the shared values of the school community and which are owned by the whole school are likely to be more effective.

- Acceptable behaviour is more likely if there are clear routines and procedures governing teaching and learning within the classroom and activities outside the classroom.

- All members of the school community need to own and understand the framework of rewards, sanctions and punishments.

- There is a clear relationship between success in learning, high self-esteem and appropriate behaviour.

- Teachers with high self-esteem enable their pupils to raise their self-esteem.

- School staff who are able to reflect positively on their own practice and who feel supported by their Senior Management Team (SMT) and their colleagues, are more likely to have high self-esteem.

- Staff need to feel confident that they have a range of strategies available to deal with particularly difficult behaviour within the framework of an overall policy.

- There is considerable expertise within the staff of each school which should be shared.

Chapters 2–9 raise issues which schools need to consider in their review and development of a whole-school behaviour policy.

Chapter 2

Teaching and learning

Children who behave inappropriately in the teaching and learning situation have often failed in personal relationships and in learning.

The relationship between teacher and child is a very special one, founded on mutual respect and trust. The situation can be likened to the nurturing relationship between a parent/carer and child where the parent/carer nurtures the child and the child feeds and grows emotionally and physically.

Where a child feels he or she has 'failed' in the parent/carer–child or adult–child relationship, the effect is to lower the child's self-esteem. The child is now wary of relating to other adults because of the residual pain of having 'failed' in previous relationships. Teachers cannot understand why they, as 'nice' professional adults, cannot get a positive response from this child and tend to take any inappropriate behaviour as being aimed at them personally. It is easy to forget that it takes a long time to overcome what has taken a long time to create.

Workers in the field of emotional and behavioural difficulties have tended to assume that there is a link between self-esteem and behavioural difficulties. It has appeared self-evident that these children have a poor opinion of themselves and low self-confidence: for example, they often describe themselves and their work as 'rubbish'. However, this link between low self-esteem and emotional and behavioural difficulties has been largely anecdotal. There have been very few studies into the self-esteem of children with emotional and behavioural difficulties apart from Lund (1987), who found that the self-esteem of children attending Northamptonshire's schools for children with emotional and behavioural difficulties was significantly lower than that of the school-aged population as a whole.

In addition, children who consistently fail to achieve academically also tend to have lower self-esteem. There have been several studies which have demonstrated this; for example, Lawrence (1973) reported the effects of increasing self-esteem on reading skills. He found that poor readers improved their reading skills to a greater extent if they were 'counselled' than if they received remedial reading help. This is not surprising because, in simple terms, the starting point for achievement is a mind uncluttered by worries. West *et al.* (in Lawrence, 1987) reviewed several studies and found a correlation of 0.13 to 0.50 between academic achievement and self-esteem. Two further researchers found that:

> Students able to meet the academic expectations of schools are likely to develop positive attitudes towards themselves as learners and those who fail are likely to develop negative feelings.   (Purkey and Novak, 1984, p.28)

There is a great deal of confusion about self-concept and self-esteem. In general:

- the *self* is that part of ourselves of which we are conscious – 'me';

- *self-concept* (sometimes referred to as self-image) is our *idea* of ourselves as a person – we use it to define the kind of person we are and to evaluate our behaviour;

- *self-esteem* is the value we place on ourselves – what we feel about ourselves. It is high self-esteem which is at the centre of achievement in learning and behaviour

Self-esteem is influenced by the messages a person receives back from *significant others* in response to their behaviour.

Children tend to have high self-esteem and to feel secure when the messages they receive from significant others in their lives tell them that they are valued and cared about. Consequently, the self-esteem of young children is influenced by the feedback they receive from parents or carers – the most significant others in their lives at that stage. Children with low self-esteem have often suffered ongoing rejection or indifference, are uncertain as to their values and standards, and have feelings of deficiency and weakness (Coopersmith, 1967).

In early schooling, children tend to focus on the aspects of the school which mean most to them to date: play and 'nice' adults (Beane and Lipka, 1984), and teachers become significant others in their lives. In later childhood, other children in the peer group begin to assume greater importance. The adolescent faces an 'identity crisis' (Erikson, 1968) and can be highly concerned about what others think about him or her. The pupils' peers then become significant others. It is desirable that pupils receive positive messages from the significant others within the school community.

Self-esteem is an essential issue within any system for assessing the individual needs of pupils, individual education plans and target-setting, and these are referred to in more depth in Chapter 3, Rewards and sanctions, and in Chapter 9, The difficult pupil. In general, a whole-school behaviour policy cannot be effective unless the enhancement of the self-esteem of all members of the school community is at its core.

There is an implication here that pupils should be enabled to succeed in learning and in behaviour all the time, but this is not possible. We all make mistakes as part of growing up. At the same time, certain subjects, like science, mathematics and design and technology have elements of investigative learning which can depend on finding out answers which are 'wrong'.

Pupils will not attempt to try work unless they know that it is all right to fail in these circumstances. On the other hand, failure must not be a learning experience which damages their self-esteem.

Classroom management

Most of the published ideas and research into effective control of behaviour focus on the interaction between teacher and child within a system of classroom organization and management. There is little attempt to link effective teaching through the curriculum to the management of individual children's behaviour within the classroom.

The way the curriculum is organized and presented is of crucial importance in stimulating interest, creating relevance and enabling the child to succeed in learning and in adult–child relationships. This in turn reinforces the process of self-esteem enhancement and emotional adjustment (see Chapter 8, Support for all). Positive behaviour management should be an integral part of curriculum planning (see page 29).

Teachers have differing perceptions of incidents of inappropriate behaviour: One teacher might see a particular behaviour as deviant and therefore unacceptable, whereas another teacher might see it as a normal and rational reaction to intolerable stresses within that pupil's life and as such, acceptable behaviour. For the individual concerned, the behaviour may be acceptable but at the same time, as behaviour within a group, it might be unacceptable.

Inappropriate behaviour can also lead to 'labelling'. The pupil who exhibits intolerable behaviour is often rejected by the adults within the school community and the current high levels of exclusions (see page 2) have resulted from this. Teachers who are operating under extreme stress tend to have low self-esteem and do not have the emotional energy to look beyond the surface behaviour of their pupils.

Hargreaves *et al.* (1975) talk about 'deviance provocative' and 'deviance insulative' teachers:

A 'deviance provocative' teacher finds that:
– deviant pupils behave in highly deviant ways in the classroom and his handling of them serves to exacerbate their deviance.   (p.260)

A 'deviance insulative' teacher finds that:
– the same pupils present relatively few problems in his classroom and his handling of them seems to inhibit their deviance.   (p.260)

A summary of the characteristics of 'deviance provocative' and 'deviance insulative' teachers, taken from Hargreaves *et al.* (1975), may be found in Table 2.1.

Table 2.1 *Characteristics of 'deviance provocative' and 'deviance insulative' teachers*

DEVIANCE PROVOCATIVE TEACHERS	DEVIANCE INSULATIVE TEACHERS
• Believe that deviant pupils do not want to work and will do everything to avoid it • It is impossible to provide conditions under which they will work • If they are ever to work then the pupils must change	• Believe that deviant pupils really want to work • If the pupils do not work the conditions are assumed to be at fault • These conditions can be changed and it is their responsibility to initiate that change
• Are unable to defuse difficult situations • Ultimatums are frequently issued, leading to confrontations	• Avoid confrontations
• Give preferential treatment to conformist pupils	• Make an effort to avoid any kind of favouritism or preferential treatment
• See discipline as a contest and one which must be won • Consider the deviant pupils to be anti-authority and are confident that they are determined not to conform to classroom rules • Refer pupils to a higher authority when they refuse to comply	• Are firm with the pupils, believing that this is what they prefer • Base discipline on a clear set of classroom rules which are made explicit to the pupils

• Are fatalistic • Expect pupils to behave badly • Blame them for their misconduct • Believe that they are resistant and hostile and committed to their deviance • See pupils as potential saboteurs and do not believe that any signs of improvement are authentic • Make negative evaluative comments to them	• Are highly optimistic • Assume that pupils will behave well and cooperate with them • Encourage any signs of improvement • Respect and care about deviant pupils and tell them that they do
• Ignore deviant pupils in lessons	• See all pupils as potential contributors to the lesson
• Dislike the deviant pupils and feel themselves unfortunate in having to teach them	• Claim to like all children and consider working with them a privilege
• Denigrate and laugh at pupils	• Rarely make negative comments about pupils who misbehave • Allow the pupils to save face when they are punished
• Are suspicious of them because their experience has taught them not to trust them	• Trust them
• Avoid contact with pupils outside the classroom	• Enjoy meeting the pupils informally outside the classroom where they can joke with them and take an interest in their personal problems
• Make negative evaluative comments about deviant pupils in the staffroom	• Often spring to the defence of pupils who are being discussed in the staffroom

From information in Hargreaves *et al.* (1975)

In practice of course, teachers come somewhere on a continuum between the two extremes and where they come at any one time can depend on how they feel, what they are teaching and who they are teaching.

This is not a book about classroom management as such, although effective procedures for management in the classroom are essential to any whole-school behaviour policy. Smith and Laslett (1993) in their book, *Effective Classroom Control*, suggest a positive regime in the classroom, based on 'Four rules of classroom management':

Rule one: Get them in
This is divided into 'greeting, seating and starting'.

Rule two: Get them out
This concerns concluding a lesson and dismissing a class.

Rule three: Get on with it
This concerns the content of the lesson and the way it is organized and the style of teaching and learning.

Rule four: Get on with them
This emphasizes the importance of knowing each individual pupil and their strengths and weaknesses but it does not acknowledge the relationship between styles of teaching and learning, academic success and motivation to learn, on the one hand, and disaffection on the other.

They stress that teachers who have definite routines and who insist on those routines, seem to establish a more secure working environment for their pupils, with consequently less inappropriate behaviour.

Routines

If all teachers and pupils within the school community share common routines in the process of teaching and learning, this in itself promotes a stable learning environment and consequent appropriate behaviour. Any inconsistency in approaches between teachers has the effect of promoting insecurity and unsettled behaviour. Under such circumstances, learning becomes much more difficult.

Routines offer safety and also a framework in which the child can work. To know that he or she always enters the classroom in the same way and settles to work in the same way enables the habit of working to become part of the routine.

> Routines regulate the flow of activities within the classroom and provide a predictable pattern and sequence for learning experiences. They should mark out the phases or stages of a lesson, so that a demonstration or talk is followed by practice, with settled arrangements for distributing and collecting materials, moving around the room and seeking help and advice when needed.
>
> (Cooper *et al.*, 1994, p.121)

For children who behave inappropriately, they offer a framework of security in which they can relate to adults and achieve in learning and behaviour.

The extent to which this can happen will depend on the size of the school. Small schools could ensure that most classroom routines are shared, whereas in large schools there could be specific routines within departments, but perhaps only the routines of entering and leaving the classroom, responding to achievement in learning and behaviour and some rewards and sanctions can be common throughout the school. It often helps if the routines are incorporated into rules for each classroom which have been developed by the pupils and teachers together.

The effective teacher also knows the importance of reinforcing success through the routine of celebrating achievement. It is important that targets in learning and behaviour should be realistic for each child so that all children have a chance of having their success celebrated. This is discussed in more detail in Chapter 3, Rewards and sanctions, and in Chapter 9, The difficult pupil.

Promoting appropriate behaviour in the classroom

The following methods have been found to be effective strategies:

Do...

- Have the work well prepared, including specially differentiated materials for *all* pupils. Pupils often behave inappropriately because they are bored or under-challenged, or if they find the work irrelevant or difficult.

- Make sure the room is laid out as you want it and that all the materials and equipment are ready for use.

- Establish and insist on routines for:
  - entering the classroom,
  - putting bags and coats away,
  - seating arrangements,
  - explaining the tasks ahead,
  - equipment needed,
  - giving out work/books,
  - setting out work,
  - listening to the teacher,
  - listening to other pupils,
  - questions and answers,
  - cooperative work,
  - stopping work,

- summarizing the session,
- giving out homework,
- leaving the classroom to go to the toilet,
- clearing up,
- packing up and leaving the classroom,
- using support staff in the classroom.

- Know and use the pupils' first names.

- Treat the pupils as responsible and valued human beings.

- Establish positive norms of behaviour with clear expectations for the group as a whole and for the individuals within it – 'This is how we behave in here'.

- Concentrate on the work in hand.

- Ignore inappropriate behaviour as far as possible.

- Praise and encourage those who are working well.

- Use eye contact or a hand gesture to express disapproval.

- Have a quiet word with the pupil that the behaviour is inappropriate and should stop.

- Try to maintain a good level of humour – learning is fun!

- Describe the effects of the behaviour not the behaviour itself. ('When you call out it disturbs the others', 'When you make a noise the class can't hear', etc).

- Send for help in good time.

- Ask for a pupil to be withdrawn (have 'time-out'; see Chapter 3, Rewards and sanctions).

- Allow time for a pupil to unwind before he or she is asked to make amends.

- Follow up any inappropriate behaviour with the pupil on their own.

Don't...

- Start the lesson until all the pupils are ready.

- Talk above the background noise.

- Shout.

- Make sarcastic or hurtful comments about pupils.

- Deal with disruptive behaviour or set targets for behaviour in front of other pupils.

- Allow pupils to sit where they want to.

- Allow pupils to wear coats or keep bags on the work tables.

- Finish the lesson in a rush without summarizing what has been covered.

- Draw unnecessary attention to inappropriate behaviour.

- Provoke confrontations.

- Make any physical contact with the pupils.

- Interview a pupil in a closed room alone.

These established practices are going to be much more effective if they are practised by the whole staff and incorporated into the whole-school behaviour policy.

Information about managing particularly difficult behaviour within the classroom may be found in Chapter 9, The difficult pupil.

Differentiation and inappropriate behaviour

Differentiation involves adapting the content and process of teaching and learning to meet the learning needs of all pupils within a teaching group. The National Curriculum Council (NCC) saw differentiation as:

> the process by which curriculum objectives, teaching methods, assessment methods, resources and learning activities are planned to cater for the needs of individual pupils. (NCC, 1991)

> The matching of work to the abilities of individual children, so that they are stretched, but still achieve success. (NCC, 1993)

Visser's definition (1993, p.15) seems better suited to teaching style and methods:

> Differentiation is the process whereby teachers meet the need for progress through the curriculum by selecting appropriate teaching methods to match an individual child's learning strategies, within a group situation.

In its handbooks, *Guidance on the Inspection of Nursery and Primary Schools* (OFSTED, 1995a), *Guidance on the Inspection of Secondary Schools* (OFSTED, 1995b), and *Guidance on the Inspection of Special Schools* (OFSTED, 1995c), OFSTED does not mention the word 'differentiation'. However, the three handbooks give slightly different guidelines on what is to be evaluated and reported on in Section 5.1, 'Teaching':

Inspectors must evaluate and report on:

- the quality of teaching and its contribution to pupils' attainment and progress highlighting;
- (iii) the extent to which teaching promotes the learning of all pupils, paying particular attention to any pupils who have special educational needs or for whom English is an additional language. (OFSTED, 1995a, p.66)
- (iii) the extent to which the teaching meets the needs of all pupils, paying particular attention to any pupils who have special educational needs or for whom English is an additional language. (OFSTED, 1995b, p.70)
- (iii) the extent to which the teaching promotes the learning of all pupils (OFSTED, 1995c, p.68).

A comprehensive review of the concept and principles of differentiation has been provided by the National Curriculum Council for teachers of science and the following is taken directly from *Science and Pupils with Special Educational Needs* (NCC, 1991, pp.2–3):

Differentiation is the process by which curriculum objectives, teaching methods, assessment methods, resources and learning activities are planned to cater for the needs of individual pupils.

Differentiated activities
A curriculum which is differentiated for every pupil will:
- build on past achievements
- present challenges to allow for more achievements
- provide opportunity for success
- remove barriers to participation.

Teachers use two main ways of differentiating learning activities:

Differentiation by task
After establishing curriculum objectives for a class activity, the next step is to develop tasks which help individual pupils achieve these objectives. There are many factors which affect the difficulty of the task. These include:
- how familiar the pupils are with the materials and apparatus to be used
- how familiar the pupils are with the concepts and vocabulary involved in the investigation
- the required accuracy for measurements
- the number and type of variables involved in an investigation
- the extent to which the teacher leads or prompts pupils.

Differentiation by outcomes
This involves setting a common task for the class. The task is designed so that every pupil understands what is required of them. They use their knowledge and understanding to achieve success at different levels. The more able may be expected to:
- use more difficult concepts in planning investigations
- plan and carry out more complex investigations
- complete more stages in an investigation

- make more measurements
- measure more accurately
- record results more precisely
- express findings in more sophisticated vocabulary.

Most teachers differentiate the *content* of the curriculum. Here, it is the resources of materials and equipment which are crucially linked to differentiation. However, in order to motivate each child and to involve each one in learning experiences which are perceived as personally relevant, it is necessary to differentiate the *process* of teaching and learning. Here it is the resources of adult support, in particular teaching support, which are crucially linked to differentiation.

The response to most assessments of special educational needs through the *Code of Practice* (DfE, 1994b) is additional teaching help. This might well provide useful support to a child with learning difficulties, but ten hours' support from an adult sitting alongside a pupil with behaviour problems in a mainstream classroom is not going to help differentiate the process of teaching and learning within that group so as to make it relevant to that pupil. A much more radical approach of providing extra teaching help is required.

Differentiation and emotional and behavioural difficulties

The most extreme example of differentiating the curriculum, as far as behaviour is concerned, can be found in a good special school for children who have emotional and behavioural difficulties. Children with emotional and behavioural difficulties have low self-esteem resulting from a failure in learning and in relationships. Because of this:

- They are reluctant to commit themselves to anything which might lead to further failure. Adults have let them down and so they do not trust teachers not to 'set them up' to fail. They know that people 'do not like them' and so they have nothing to lose by opting out.

- They are often emotionally immature and are only motivated by what they see as personally relevant and offering immediate reward. They cannot cooperate with others.

- Their minds are full of worries and they have little emotional energy left for learning. Their stamina and concentration is poor.

In order to respond to these needs, the specialist teacher of children with emotional and behavioural difficulties manages the process of teaching and learning in the following ways:

- Work is broken into small stages and if it is noticed that the children are not understanding, the work is presented from a different angle, without making it appear that the child should have been able to do it the other way.

- Success is reinforced at every stage by praise, encouragement, display work and by involving other adults to take an interest in the work and to show approval of it. Even so, there can be the odd occasion when a child pronounces that a piece of work is 'rubbish' and tears it up. Sometimes, the teacher will rescue the pieces and carefully stick them back together later, pointing out how 'awful' it is to destroy your own work.

- Often, the child cannot face any relationship between adult and child. The teacher uses Information Technology to make the process less personal and to give space between him or her and the child.

- One of the consequences of low self-esteem is the inability to concentrate on anything outside the here and now. Learning experiences therefore need to be perceived as personally relevant at that particular moment. The teacher also gives immediate, positive feedback.

- These children find difficulty in sharing and in cooperative work. The teacher allows group work to grow out of individual working and gives opportunities for working together in a way which does not mean that one child is dependent on or in competition with another. For example, the whole group might be making a model of a Roman town, with each child making a different building.

- The teacher persists in trying to interest the child, even when it is obvious that he or she has insufficient emotional energy to pay attention to the topic in hand. The child is given space and the opportunity to be included in the teaching and learning at an appropriate time. Often, the teacher is able to put the learning into a different mode; for example using the computer or drawing instead of writing. The skilled teacher appears to know the right moment and the right approach and keeps on trying from his or her repertoire until an approach interests and motivates the child.

- The teacher works with the group more as a group leader than a directing teacher – from within the group rather than from the outside.

- The teacher talks to the children about the theoretical (or knowledge) element of the project and discusses ideas about it when the children are involved in practical activities. For example, a lot of information can be discussed and apparently understood and retained, when the whole group, including the teacher, are involved in practical activities, like model-making.

- These children find written work difficult because they prefer not to record what they perceive or anticipate as failure. They also find difficulty in abstract concepts, which they tend to see as not relevant to their current situation. The teacher tries to make the learning practical and hands-on.

- The project work is reinforced by using associated subject areas. Through this process they can also use the skills they have acquired in these subjects. The children can also gain status and confidence by demonstrating their knowledge to the rest of the school community.

- Any teaching and learning with children with emotional and behavioural difficulties takes much longer than it does in a mainstream school. (For this reason, terminal examinations discriminate against these children.) For the teacher, this skilled and specialized differentiation of the curriculum is very time-consuming. The teacher needs to prepare several parallel lessons for virtually every session, for individual children and with differing approaches.

To summarize, teachers in schools for children with emotional and behavioural difficulties:

- make success in learning more probable than failure;
- use a wide variety of learning materials;
- develop a number of different teaching approaches within each lesson;
- reinforce learning through topic work and cross-curricular themes;
- work *with* the children rather than direct the children;
- make learning practical and hands-on wherever possible;
- allow space between the teacher and child by using Information Technology;
- ensure that the child perceives the learning as personally relevant;
- are sensitive to the emotional energy of the child;
- allow time.

While it is not suggested that these techniques would all be appropriate in mainstream primary and secondary schools, they do perhaps illustrate the range of strategies which are available for all teachers to use, as they feel appropriate.

Chapter 3

Rewards and sanctions

Pupils who are motivated to learn and involved in the teaching and learning process tend to behave appropriately. Pupils who are bored by what they are taught and cannot see its relevance to them, tend to behave inappropriately.

The importance of self-esteem has already been stressed in Chapter 2, Teaching and learning. Pupils with high self-esteem tend to behave appropriately; pupils with low self-esteem tend to behave inappropriately. Self-esteem can be increased by mutual respect between teachers and pupils and by the positive effects of deserved praise and encouragement. Put another way: children who are treated like rubbish, behave like rubbish.

Pupils respond better in the teaching and learning situation if they are given tasks which they recognize as personally achievable. This has implications for the differentiation of the curriculum for each pupil as well as for the school's behaviour policy (see Chapter 2, Teaching and learning).

Pupils need to know exactly what behaviour is appropriate and what behaviour is inappropriate and the kind of acceptable standards in learning and in behaviour to which they should be aspiring. They should be set targets which they perceive as achievable. This setting of targets for learning and for behaviour (see below) should be an integral part of teaching and learning and of the pupils' Records of Achievement. At the same time, they need to know the rewards they will receive if their behaviour is appropriate and the sanctions which will be imposed if their behaviour is inappropriate.

The celebration and reward of achievement

The effective teacher knows the importance of reinforcing success through celebrating and rewarding achievement.

Procedure for celebrating achievement
(Note that not all are appropriate to all phases):

- making a child aware of success throughout each lesson
- talking about successes at the end of the lesson
- positive comments in an 'Achievement Book'
- asking the child to show their work/Achievement Book to a visitor or a senior member of staff
- pointing out achievement to the rest of the group
- taking work or the Achievement Book or a note home to parents/carers
- a 'mention' in assembly or tutor group/class meeting
- charts on the wall
- work displayed
- photographs and/or videos
- a personal 'Record of Achievement Book'
- awarding certificates.

Rewards are more likely to be effective if:

- they are meaningful to the child (and not embarrassing)
- they are given immediately
- it is clear what the rewards are for
- they are related to appropriate behaviour which is accepted as such by the child
- they relate to small target steps in achievement
- the targets for learning and behaviour are agreed between teacher and child and reviewed regularly.

Targets

Adults tend to define inappropriate behaviour in emotive terms and consequently find it difficult to set targets for appropriate behaviour. They tend to use blanket terms to describe a child's behaviour: 'He's a nuisance'; 'She's attention seeking'; 'He's careless'; 'She's a stirrer', and so on.

It is more useful in analysing behaviour and setting targets, to *describe the behaviour in terms of what the child has been observed doing*: 'He shouts out loud in the middle of class reading'; 'She leaves her place and hangs around my table'; 'He keeps forgetting his books'; 'She waits until another child has done something wrong and then tells everyone about it'. Once behaviour has been described in these terms, it is easier to set targets, as shown in Table 3.1.

Table 3.1 *Setting targets*

Inappropriate behaviour	Targets
Ian shouts out loud in the middle of class reading	1. Ian will sit quietly during story 2. Ian will put his hand up if he wants to tell the teacher something 3. Ian will put his hand down if the teacher is busy
Dierdre leaves her place and stands near to the teacher's table	1. Dierdre will stay in her place 2. Dierdre will put up her hand if she wants to talk to the teacher 3. Dierdre will wait if the teacher is busy
Bevan keeps forgetting to bring books to school	1. Bevan will try to get hold of a school bag 2. Bevan will make a list of the books he takes home each day 3. Bevan will check the list at home before he leaves for school
Kali waits until another child does something wrong and then tells everyone else about it	1. Kali will ignore what others are doing

Remember:

- the process of setting targets should be agreed between all members of staff

- each child should have individual targets

- children must be involved in setting their own targets

- targets should be set for achieving appropriate behaviour, not for stopping the inappropriate behaviour

- targets should be realistic and not intimidating: the child will reject any target he or she sees as unobtainable.

- use several targets to provide small steps for putting things right, where appropriate.

- a senior member of staff should monitor target-setting in order to achieve consistency.

A blank grid for target-setting may be found in Table 3.2. (See Chapter 9, The difficult pupil, for setting targets with children who have more overt behavioural difficulties.)

Table 3.2 *A grid for setting targets*

TARGET-SETTING	
Inappropriate behaviour	Targets

Rewards

The teacher can reward personally and immediately by:

- encouraging
- smiling and nodding
- a positive tone of voice
- praise
- being near to the pupil
- making positive comments on work.

The teacher can also reward by giving:

- special privileges
- trophies
- choosing favourite activities
- extra play/break time (primary or special schools).

Alternatively, the teacher could award something which conveys approval and status:

- badges
- merit awards

- certificates
- team/house points
- photographs.

Material rewards

Some schools, especially special schools, go one step further and award 'points' for appropriate behaviour which can be exchanged for material rewards. If these are 'fair', ie, each pupil's targets have been set according to their needs, then every pupil should achieve the same material rewards. Pupils learn that in order to gain a material reward they must achieve in learning or in behaviour, but they also learn that they do not have to make any effort to achieve in those aspects of learning and behaviour for which they are not materially rewarded. Where is the incentive to do something for the benefit of themselves, for other individuals or for the good of the school community? The problem with these so-called 'token economies' is that they appeal to children's greed and do not promote values of caring and cooperation. ('If I don't get something for it, I don't do it'.)

A framework for rewards in learning and behaviour

Pupils should be rewarded for meeting targets in:

- changing inappropriate behaviour into appropriate behaviour
- achievement in learning.

Rewards can be organized in a series of *levels*:

Level 1: Praise and encouragement

- to the pupil
- involving any adults visiting the group (mainly primary and special)
- in assembly/class meeting
- a phone call/letter home to parents/carers (see Chapter 7, Involving parents, for suggestions on how schools should communicate with parents).

Level 2: Merits

- certificates
- tokens
- comments in a book
- comments on a chart on the wall

The merits will be:

- mentioned in assembly or class meeting
- stamped with a symbol or have a sticky stamp affixed by a senior member of staff
- recorded on a chart on the wall of the tutor/classroom
- taken home to show parents/carers.

Level 3: Certificates of achievement

These will be awarded for ten merits and:

- will be presented in assembly
- will be copied for display in the tutor/classroom
- will be copied to take home to parents/carers
- the child will be photographed with the certificate and the photograph displayed in the entrance area of the school and a copy taken home
- will be put into the pupil's Record of Achievement file.

Remember: if the pupils' targets are set at the right level for each pupil then every pupil should regularly meet the targets set and hence achieve rewards.

Individual Education Plans

Pupils who have Individual Education Plans (IEPs), based on the *Code of Practice on the Identification and Assessment of Special Educational Needs* (DfE, 1994b), could have achievements noted on their IEPs (see Chapter 9, The difficult pupil, for more information on IEPs).

Sanctions

If the ethos of the classroom and the school is positive then there will already be an atmosphere of mutual respect and self-esteem in which children are behaving appropriately and teaching and learning is leading to achievement. Part of this depends on establishing routines and appropriate rewards, as has already been mentioned; the other part is a system of sanctions which are clearly understood and consistently applied so that teachers and pupils know exactly where they stand.

Often, the undesirable behaviour will stop if the pupil perceives that other pupils are behaving appropriately and are obtaining attention by so doing. Teachers should try to ignore the pupil who is misbehaving but draw attention to the behaviour which is appropriate, including the occasional appropriate behaviour from the pupil in question.

The way in which teachers respond to inappropriate behaviour is crucial.

The key is to accept the pupil as a person whilst making it clear that the behaviour is unacceptable:

> *Separate the pupil from the behaviour:*
> *'We want you, we do not want this behaviour'.*

An important part of caring is control, and pupils with few inner controls need the security of external controls. In practice, pressed to the ultimate of physical control, this can provide the controlling teacher with a dilemma if he or she is to protect him or herself from allegations of assault. However, in English law, the welfare of the child is paramount and caring adults in charge of children (*in loco parentis*) must take whatever steps they feel are appropriate to safeguard the well-being of the child in his or her care (see Chapter 5, Pupil and staff protection).

Sanctions are more effective than punishments with pupils who exhibit more disturbing behaviour as a result of having failed in adult–child relationships. The teacher is just one more adult who is likely to let them down. Punishment, in these circumstances, cannot be the right response to inappropriate behaviour. In a situation of developing acceptance, trust and security, it is seen by the pupil as a betrayal by the punishing adult. It is rejecting and reinforces the pupil's deep-seated belief that adults reject them because they are bad – like their behaviour (see Chapter 9, The difficult pupil).

Pupils often exhibit inappropriate behaviour because they have low self-esteem; they are 'rubbish' in their eyes. This view of themselves is based on how others have responded to their behaviour in the past: If people are treated like rubbish, they feel like rubbish and they behave like rubbish. If the adult gives up, the pupil will think, 'I knew I was no good', and behave accordingly (see Chapter 2, Teaching and learning).

This does not mean that the pupil should be *'allowed to get away with it'*. All pupils must be confronted with the unacceptable nature of their behaviour and sanctions should be imposed in order to get the pupil to recognize the behaviour as unreasonable and unacceptable and to make some attempt to make amends:

> *'OK, this is what you have done...'*
> *'What should you have done?'*
> *'What are you going to do in future?' (and, as appropriate),*
> *'How are you going to put things right?'*

Possibilities for *'putting things right'* could be negotiated in line with the pupil's behaviour targets. Putting things right (reparation) might include:

- apologizing
- making up lost work in free time
- repairing damage caused.

Whatever other considerations apply, sanctions imposed too long after an 'offence' or for too long, simply reinforce resentment and the pupil's feelings of badness and rejection. After a while, ongoing sanctions do not mean anything.

Sanctions should be:

- immediate
- related to the behavioural targets of that pupil
- focused on the behaviour, not on the pupil as a person
- perceived as fair
- geared to giving an opportunity for putting things right (reparation), bearing in mind the pupil's capabilities.

Afterwards:

- the slate should be wiped clean
- a fresh start should be made by all concerned.

Note: sanctions should always be administered in as 'antiseptic' a manner as possible – not in haste nor in anger.

Withdrawal

Withdrawal (or 'time out') can be used as an effective way of helping a pupil recognize his or her inappropriate behaviour as a problem, and to come to terms with it. It emphasizes the responsibility of the individual to the group ethos.

Withdrawal should only be used as an integral part of an overall behaviour management policy, based on shared values and well-established procedures for behaviour management within the teaching or activity group. If this is not so, then it could be perceived by the pupil as a punishment.

Appropriate behaviour within the teaching or activity group is crucially linked to teaching and learning. Very few pupils who are motivated and involved in learning behave inappropriately (see Chapter 2, Teaching and learning). Withdrawal should be set within this context and should only be used for those pupils who affect the learning of others to a serious extent.

Conditions for withdrawal

- the teaching or activity group must be seen as a more desirable place to be than the place to which the pupil is withdrawn.

- it must be as 'antiseptic' as possible *(not in haste nor in anger)*

- there should not be an audience

- attention-seeking should not be rewarded

- it should not make the pupil appear a martyr, either to other pupils or to the pupil's family

- it should be for the shortest possible time

- it should be complete in itself

- it should be done by a 'teacher on call' or a member of the Senior Management Team.

Procedure for withdrawal

1. Discuss the undesirability of the behaviour with the pupil and request that it stop:
   - 'This is what you are doing'
   - 'It is disturbing others'
   - 'Please stop'.

2. If the undesirable behaviour continues, the pupil should be warned that if he or she does not stop, they will have to be withdrawn:
   - 'You are still disturbing the group. If you continue, you will have to go out'.
     Care should be taken that this is not said as if it is a punishment.

3. If the undesirable behaviour still continues, assistance should be sought from the teacher on call or a member of the SMT. That person will remove the pupil from the room.

4. If the pupil is in a calm state and simply needs a period of 'time-out', he or she can sit in a suitable room. (Although this is difficult in some schools this should ideally be one with no audience, which is quiet and which offers as little stimulation as possible). If he or she is in an angry or distressed state, he or she needs to be supervised by an adult.

   If any form of physical restraint is necessary, the school's, Local Education Authority's and Department for Education and Employment's official policies and guidelines on physical control and restraint should be followed rigorously (see Chapter 5, Pupil and staff protection).

5. *Wait* until the pupil is able to talk about his or her behaviour in the lesson or activity with the supervising adult: sooner or later they will be able to do so. The following should be discussed:
   - what the inappropriate behaviour was
   - what would have been the appropriate behaviour

Figure 3.1 *Steps in the withdrawal procedure*

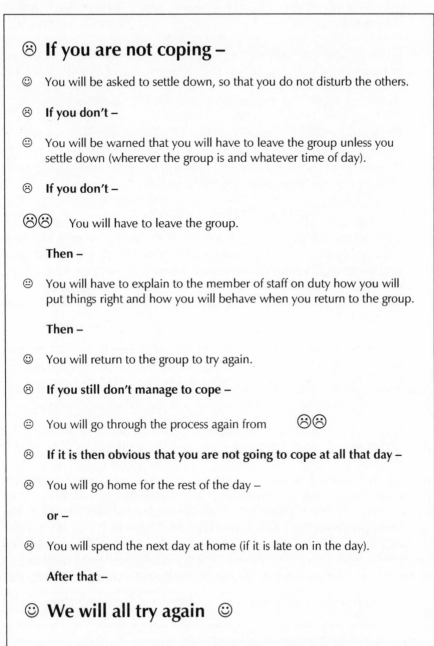

☹ **If you are not coping –**

☺ You will be asked to settle down, so that you do not disturb the others.

☹ **If you don't –**

☺ You will be warned that you will have to leave the group unless you settle down (wherever the group is and whatever time of day).

☹ **If you don't –**

☹☹ You will have to leave the group.

Then –

☺ You will have to explain to the member of staff on duty how you will put things right and how you will behave when you return to the group.

Then –

☺ You will return to the group to try again.

☹ **If you still don't manage to cope –**

☺ You will go through the process again from ☹☹

☹ **If it is then obvious that you are not going to cope at all that day –**

☹ You will go home for the rest of the day –

or –

☹ You will spend the next day at home (if it is late on in the day).

After that –

☺ **We will all try again** ☺

  - how things can be put right
  - how he or she will behave when they return to the lesson or activity.

6. When the pupil returns to the group, the teacher should welcome him or her back and the incident is then *closed* (if it is at change of teacher time, the pupils should be taken to the withdrawing teacher in order to 'put things right' with him or her before going on to the next lesson).

7. If the same pupil is obviously unable to settle in the lesson or activity without seriously affecting the learning or behaviour of the other pupils that day, he or she should be taken home for the rest of the day (or remain at home the next day, if it is late on in the day):
  - 'I am sorry but that behaviour is not acceptable because (give reasons) and you will have to go home'.

Note: any sending home must be arranged with the parents/carers (see Chapter 7, Involving parents). Care must be taken to ensure that the pupil is not manipulating the situation in order to be sent home.

8. When the pupil returns to school, the points outlined in 5 (above), should be repeated.

9. Incidents should be recorded in the school's 'Incident book' or 'Day book'.[1]

A flowchart like the one in Figure 3.1 (p.41) (which is possibly more geared to primary and special schools) could be placed on the wall of each teaching area.

Punishments

It should be possible to organize rewards and sanctions as part of a system of positive behaviour management, as outlined in the first part of this chapter, without recourse to punishment. Strategies suggested in Chapter 9, The difficult pupil, should also be taken into account.

Punishments do not work, either as means of preventing further inappropriate behaviour (or no one would repeat it after being punished) or as a deterrent (otherwise others would not exhibit that inappropriate behaviour).

Punishment is degrading, breeds resentment and lowers self-esteem.

However, teachers often feel that they must demonstrate that they are in control: they feel that punishments demonstrate that control, and act as a deterrent to other pupils. It must also be pointed out that teachers often feel aggrieved by the way in which they have been treated by pupils and want demonstrable revenge against them. Teachers are also human and prone to hold grudges like everyone else; 'Ah yes, you were a real pain last lesson – sit there where I can see you!'.

It is essential, in any system of positive behaviour management, that each incident is dealt with as soon as possible – and the slate wiped clean.

In a school which has shared positive values about the individuals within the school community and the way in which they should be treated, this problem is less frequent. Teachers are more willing to deal with behaviour problems as part of an overall whole-school behaviour policy and to treat each incident as complete in itself. They are also more able to separate the pupil from the behaviour. The resolution of inappropriate behaviour becomes a learning experience at which the pupil can succeed, feel a sense of achievement and increase in self-esteem.

If there must be punishments, then these should be administered in as positive a way as possible:

Lines
Lines should not be frivolous or offensive. They should relate in some way to the inappropriate behaviour and be as 'antiseptic' as possible.

Work around the school
It is questionable if a pupil will keep the school any tidier if made to pick up litter, but it does help to keep the school looking good.

Extra school work
Disaffected pupils are not likely to become more motivated to school work if they are given more of it. On the other hand, if the pupil achieves at the work task, then it can be positive.

On report
Unfortunately, reports are usually used as a record of misdemeanours and to make a spectacle of the pupil concerned. The report system can be used in a positive way to help set targets and to enable children to make amends.

Detentions
The main problem with detentions is that there tend to be a few regular teachers who make use of them and it is colleagues, especially SMT colleagues, who end up taking them. This problem can be alleviated by making sure that it is only the staff who use the system who run detentions.

Involvement of parents/carers (see also Chapter 8, Involving parents):

- Parents/carers are often only involved at crisis point. They should be involved earlier rather than later on in proceedings.

- Pupils hate and react against 'complaints' to parents/carers and parents/carers do not like to be made to feel responsible for inappropriate behaviour in school.

- Some pupils who exhibit more disturbing behaviour have a poor relationship with their parents/carers who can use a negative letter home as an excuse to further reject their children or even to physically chastise them.

- Parents/carers should be informed about punishments for more serious offences and given reasonable notice of detentions.

- Letters to parents/carers should not imply blame to them for the inappropriate behaviour.

- Informing parents/carers about inappropriate behaviour can have a deterrent effect. They should be asked for their comments, suggestions and advice.

- All letters to parents/carers should be written in positive terms.

- It should be borne in mind that parents who have to stay at home to look after excluded or withdrawn pupils can lose money from work.

Withdrawal of privileges

Pushed to its logical conclusion, the pupil who behaves inappropriately for most of the time will have no privileges and will not, for example, go on any trips. Care should be taken that the withdrawal of a privilege is the punishment for one incident; it should not be made as a result of adding up incidents. In practice, if inappropriate behaviour is dealt with positively through the setting of appropriate targets, and a fresh start made, then pupils should take part in all privileged activities – but be withdrawn from them if they demonstrate that they cannot cope with them.

Exclusions

Exclusions do not endear schools to disaffected pupils. The longer they are excluded, the longer it will take to reassimilate them. Exclusions often go on for far too long. It is the initial stage of exclusion which punishes; any prolonging leads to further disaffection. Care should be taken that the child feels that the punishment is complete in itself and that they can make a fresh stage with no recriminations when they return.

Whatever form of punishment is used:

- it should be in proportion to the incident
- it should be clearly understood and accepted by the child and his or her parents/carers – and seen as fair and reasonable
- it should be as 'antiseptic' as possible
- it should be complete in itself
- it should not increase the status of the child within the peer group or the family (for example, make him or her a martyr)
- it should be monitored by a member of the SMT to make sure that all members of staff are acting within the guidelines of the whole-school behaviour policy and are being fair and consistent
- it should be recorded in the teacher's own record book, which should be monitored by a member of the SMT (or head of department)
- serious incidents and punishments should be recorded in the school's 'Incident book' or 'Day book'.[1]

In general, punishments should not be given in anger or in haste and should be as 'antiseptic' as possible:

'You have done this…'
'You should have done this…'
'This is the punishment'.

> *Once the punishment has been administered the incident is closed and the pupil and adult concerned start again with a clean sheet.*

NOTE

1. Schools organize their record-keeping in different ways. In large schools these might be kept in years or departments, in small schools for the whole school. However the records are kept, all schools are obliged to keep records of serious incidents of abuse, injuries to staff or pupils and serious damage to property.

    These records *must* be made available for inspection by the governors, senior officials of the local authority, or OFSTED inspectors on request (see Chapter 5, Pupil and staff protection).

Chapter 4

Bullying

(Schools will want to refer also to the DfE publication, *Bullying: Don't suffer in silence*, DfE, 1994a.)

Whatever the roots of bullying, the victims suffer great distress and it can lead to a situation where they find difficulty in forming relationships and are prone to periods of depression. Bullying is extremely common, with up to 25 per cent of pupils in junior and middle schools claiming to be bullied at least once a term and 10 per cent once a week (DfE, 1994a).

What is bullying?

Bullying is a form of *aggression*, distinguished by the fact that it is repeated and that it is not normally provoked by the victim. It can take various forms, but the crucial feature is that one person, the bully (or a group of bullies), intentionally sets out to cause distress to another person, the victim (or group of victims).

- It can be encouraged by a sub-culture of violence within a community and is often located within anti-social gangs.

- Many bullies are often themselves victims of bullying in other situations and a school's bully might often be bullied by siblings, parents or carers at home.

- A teacher who bullies his or her pupils is often an inadequate person who is in turn being bullied by another adult within the community.

- Pupils who 'play up' a particular teacher could also be termed bullies.

- It can occur in all communities and at any age and between any age group.

- In schools bullying can take place between
  - pupils and pupils,
  - pupils and adults,
  - adults and adults.

- Often it appears to be condoned by the adults in charge because, 'It never did me any harm' or, 'He must have asked for it or he wouldn't be bullied' or, if we intervene, we will make it worse' or, 'If we ignore it, it will go away'.

- Bullying does not have to be physical. Often emotional abuse, based on verbal intimidation, can be even more distressing than physical abuse.

Evidence of bullying

Evidence of bullying can be gathered from a wide variety of sources, including:

- observations of behaviour throughout the school

- discussions with pupils and staff

- records from the school's 'Incident book' or 'Day book'[1]

- complaints from parents, carers or social workers

- the Survey of Bullying checklist in Figure 4.1 at the end of this chapter. (This should be given to a sample of pupils from at least one group from each year.)

Responses to bullying

By and large, the victims of bullying and their parents want the bullies to be punished, but this is not necessarily the best response. Punishment can lead to resentment and disaffection on the part of the bullies and certainly does nothing to develop their positive feelings towards their victims. If the victims think that they will be made more isolated, they will not 'tell'.

Whole-school policies which lead to an awareness of bullying as a problem in the school community and which give a chance for individual positive work with all members of the community, are much more likely to be effective. Typical of these approaches is the very effective 'No-blame' approach (Maines and Robinson, 1992).

Many schools develop separate policies for bullying but, if the school's policy for behaviour management is based on the belief that all members of the school community should treat one another with respect as individuals, then the response to bullying can be one aspect of an overall system of rewards and sanctions of the kind outlined in Chapter 3, Rewards and sanctions. There is no reason why bullying cannot be incorporated into the school's overall whole-school behaviour policy, providing the following points are taken into account:

- Schools should establish clear policies on equality of opportunity (race, gender, disability, ability) based on a shared belief within the school community that all members of the community are of equal worth, irrespective of race, gender, disability, ability, learning or behavioural difficulty, appearance, or cultural background. These should be turned into clear, owned and accepted rules about how the individuals within the community should behave towards each other (see Chapter 6, Equal opportunities).

- The affective curriculum should include, within its personal and social development programme, training on 'keeping safe' (see also Chapter 5, Pupil and staff protection). Children should also be taught how to be assertive.

- The school should regularly monitor the amount of bullying which is going on (see the checklist in Figure 4.1).

- Pupils should be encouraged to make their concerns known to a member of staff. This could form part of the 'Worry sheet' procedure (see Chapter 5, Pupil and staff protection p.58).

- Pupils should feel confident that their concerns will be taken seriously

- Staff should be careful that they treat each other with respect in front of the pupils

- Staff should treat pupils with respect and not bully them in the teaching and learning situation or around the school.

- Staff should be careful to show disapproval of the bully without bullying the bully. They should separate the pupil from the behaviour and make it clear that it is the bullying behaviour which is not wanted, and that they do want the bully.

- Bullies must be brought face-to-face with the consequences of their bullying on the victim.

- Bullies should be involved in working out how to make amends.

- Attention should be paid to helping to raise the self-esteem of bullies and victims.

- Parents/carers should be involved in seeking solutions to their children's bullying or victimization.

- A record of all bullying involving serious harassment or injuries should be maintained in the school's 'Incident book' or 'Day book'.[1]

- Education welfare officers, educational psychologists and behaviour consultants can provide advice and guidance to staff and pupils.

- An 'Awareness raising day' within the personal and social development curriculum can help pupils to become aware of:
  - different types of personality,
  - feelings,
  - what they can do,
  - it's safe to tell.

Bullied adults

Teachers with high self-esteem help to raise self-esteem in their pupils, and hence their pupils' achievements. Teachers who feel threatened and/or bullied by their senior colleagues are less likely to be able to promote appropriate behaviour in the classroom or around the school. The same applies to teachers who feel that their actions are constantly being scrutinized and graded, either within the school or by external inspectors.

School staff have a collective strength to which every member of staff contributes. If teachers feel that they are 'on trial' and unsupported by their colleagues and the SMT, they will feel that they need to look after themselves and that they have no responsibility to enable their to colleagues cope with the areas in which they are struggling: Indeed, their lack of sympathy can become overt hostility, or even bullying, as they perceive these colleagues as letting them and the school down, and giving them more work to do (see also Chapter 8, Support for all).

The whole school loses out as these isolated teachers become increasingly desperate. There can then be a tendency for them to bully the pupils as they themselves are being bullied. All members of a school community have a responsibility to support each other.

No man is an Island, entire of itself;
every man is a piece of the Continent, a part of the main,

if a clod be washed away by the sea, Europe is the less,
as well as if a promontory were,
as well as if a manor of thy friends or of thine own were;

any man's death diminishes me, because I am involved in Mankind;
And therefore never send to know for whom the bell tolls;
It tolls for thee.

(John Donne, *Meditation XVII*)

Every adult on a school staff has some particular skill or attribute which can be harnessed for the good of the school. While recognizing that they may have these particular skills, they are often totally unaware of just how good they are. It is the job of any SMT to enable each adult in the school to:

- reflect positively on their own performance (see Chapter 8, Support for all)
- recognize their strengths
- use these strengths in overcoming weaknesses in other areas
- feel useful within the school community
- feel valued within the school community.

A manager who cannot recognize and utilize any useful skills in a particular member of staff is a poor manager.

NOTE

1. Schools organize their record-keeping in different forms. In large schools these might be kept in years or departments, in small schools for the whole school. However the records are kept, all schools are obliged to keep records of serious incidents of abuse, injuries to staff or pupils and serious damage to property.

   These records *must* be made available for inspection by the governors, senior officials of the local authority, or OFSTED inspectors on request (see Chapter 5, Pupil and staff protection).

SURVEY OF BULLYING (Use this checklist ✓ to assess the degree of bullying in the school)

Read the following to each participant:

I want to find out if children are being bullied. By bullied I mean anything which is done to another person which they don't want doing to them and which makes them feel bad.

Examples might be:

calling them names – teasing – taking their things – interfering with their work – hitting them – refusing to talk to them – refusing to be with them – not letting them play – destroying their property – frightening them.

Bullying does not mean fighting with someone else of the same strength or when friends fall out.   OK?

Have you been bullied at school this term?	YES	NO	
How many times?	ONCE	TWICE	MANY
Was it by one child or by a group of children?	ONE	GROUP	
Where did it happen?			
Have you seen anyone else being bullied at school this term?	YES	NO	
How many times?	ONCE	TWICE	MANY
Was it by one child or a group of children?	ONE	GROUP	
Where did it happen?			
Have you bullied another child this term?	YES	NO	
How many times?	ONCE	TWICE	MANY
Were you on your own or with others?	OWN	GROUP	
Where did it happen?			
If you were being bullied who would you tell about it?			

Figure 4.1 *Survey of bullying checklist*

Chapter 5

Pupil and staff protection

Schools will inevitably become aware from time to time that one of their pupils is being physically, sexually or emotionally abused, or neglected. Pupils need to understand how they can protect themselves and who they can trust with confidences.

At the same time, all adults working with children are likely to be in positions where they might be accused of abusing a child. This is much more likely when the adult is exercising care and control, as required to do *in loco parentis*.

11 All schools should have procedures for handling suspected cases of abuse, including procedures to be followed if a teacher or other member of staff is accused of abuse. They should be consistent with the policies and procedures of the local ACPC (area child protection committee) and, where appropriate, the local education authority. All staff should be aware of the school's procedures, which should be easily accessible for reference.

(DfEE, 1995a, p.6)

Child abuse

Circular 10/95, *Protecting Children from Abuse* (DfEE, 1995a) contains comprehensive guidance to schools and adults working in schools. The main points it makes are:

- All staff should be alert to signs of abuse and know to whom they should report any concerns or suspicions.

- All schools and colleges should have a designated member of staff responsible for co-ordinating action within the institution and liaising with other agencies, including the Area Child Protection Committee (ACPC).

- All schools and colleges should be aware of the child protection procedures established by the ACPC and, where appropriate, the local education authority.

- All schools and colleges should have procedures (of which staff should be aware) for handling suspected cases of abuse of pupils or students, including procedures to be followed if a member of staff is accused of abuse.

- Staff with designated responsibility for child protection should receive appropriate training.

- In every local education authority a senior officer should be responsible for co-ordinating action on child protection across the authority.

(DfEE, 1995a, p.1)

The other key document to refer to in child protection is the handbook for all services, including schools, working with children: *Working Together under the Children Act 1989* (Home Office *et al.*, 1991).

Working Together gives the following definitions of abuse which are recognized for the purposes of the *Child Protection Register*, which is a register of children at risk of abuse and is maintained by the local authority social services department or by the National Society for the Prevention of Cruelty to Children (NSPCC) on behalf of the social services department:

Neglect:
The persistent or severe neglect of a child, or the failure to protect a child from exposure to any kind of danger, including cold or starvation, or extreme failure to carry out important aspects of care, resulting in the significant impairment of the child's health or development, including non-organic failure to thrive.

Physical injury:
Actual or likely physical injury to a child, or failure to prevent physical injury (or suffering) to a child including poisoning, suffocation and Munchausen's syndrome by proxy.

Sexual abuse:
Actual or likely sexual exploitation of a child or adolescent. The child may be dependent and/or developmentally immature.

Emotional abuse:
Actual or likely severe adverse effect on the emotional and behavioural development of a child caused by persistent or severe emotional ill-treatment or rejection. All abuse involves some emotional ill-treatment. This category should be used where it is the main or sole form of abuse.

Taken from Home Office *et al.*, 1991, *Working Together Under the Children Act 1989*.

6   An investigation into suspected abuse may result in a court making an emergency protection, care or supervision order if it is satisfied that the child is suffering, or is likely to suffer, 'significant harm'. 'Harm' means 'ill-treatment or the impairment of health or development' (section 31 of the Children Act 1989 (HMSO, 1989).   (DES, 1989a, p.4)

OFSTED inspects the effectiveness of the school's child protection procedures within the aspect '5.4 Support, Guidance and Pupils' Welfare'. There are 'Additional Notes' for inspectors in the three OFSTED Handbooks relating to the inspection of nursery and primary schools (OFSTED, 1995a, p.93), secondary schools (OFSTED, 1995b, p.98) and special schools (OFSTED, 1995c, p.99).

Indicators of abuse

Teachers often notice if there is something wrong with one of their pupils. They might appear out of sorts or have unexplained bruising. There are a variety of signs which *might* be indicative of abuse. *Note:* they are not in themselves proof that abuse has taken place but they should put caring adults on their guard:

Possible neglect:
- untreated injuries
- untreated illness
- excessive hunger
- poor school attendance or lateness
- undue tiredness
- running away
- low self-esteem
- drug/solvent abuse
- behaviour which is difficult to explain or out of character.

Possible physical abuse:
- obvious injuries, often with bruising
- bald patches
- scratches
- burns or scalds
- weals
- fractures in very young children.

These could be suspicious if:
- there is a reluctance to discuss injuries;
- there is a reluctance to change for PE or games;
- there is a reluctance to return home;
- the injuries are untreated;

  – the pupil is excessively aggressive;
  – improbable reasons are given for the injuries.

Possible sexual abuse:
  • sexual knowledge and/or behaviour which is inappropriate for age (including drawings)
  • reluctance to change for PE or games
  • genital irritation or inflammation
  • anxious behaviour with adults
  • timidity or withdrawal
  • seeking reassurance
  • crying easily
  • depression
  • inappropriate aggression.

Possible emotional abuse:
  • developmental immaturity
  • low self-esteem
  • speech disorders
  • wetting or soiling
  • timidity
  • over-anxiety to please
  • attention seeking
  • phased/inattentive/dream-like behaviour.

In all these cases there can often be an underachievement in learning.

What to do about suspected abuse

9   Where teachers and other staff see signs which cause them concern they should seek information from the child with tact and sympathy. It is not the responsibility of teachers and other staff in schools to investigate suspected abuse. They should not take action beyond that agreed in the procedures established by the local Area Child Protection Committee (ACPC).   (DES, 1989a, p.5)

Any adult who suspects abuse should:

  • *Listen* to what the pupil says and;

  • make detailed *factual* notes to pass on to the school's Designated Teacher (see below). A sketch showing the site and extent of any visible injuries is often useful. *Remember* that any notes might subsequently be used in criminal proceedings;

  • inform the school's Designated Teacher *immediately*.

On no account should the suspecting adult attempt to interview the pupil, examine the pupil physically, gather any other evidence or contact parents/carers. (This could have serious implications for any possible future criminal proceedings.) (See also 'Counselling' in Chapter 9, The difficult pupil, for advice on how to respond to confidences from pupils.)

Above all – do not attempt to deal with it alone – pass it on to the Designated Teacher.

The role of the Designated Teacher

Schools are required by the Children Act 1989, to appoint a member of staff, a Designated Teacher, who is responsible for monitoring child protection issues in the school, and maintaining links with the ACPC, the social services department and, where appropriate, the local education authority.

The duties of the Designated Teacher are to:

- keep records of child protection issues and concerns. (*Note*: these can be kept on computer, in which case they are exempt from the Data Protection Act 1984. The Education (School Records) Regulations 1989 exempt child protection information from disclosure although these may be required to be produced in any subsequent court proceedings);

- be aware of the signs and symptoms of abuse and when to make a referral (*when in doubt*, seek the advice of the social services department, the NSPCC or, where appropriate, the local education authority's *child protection coordinator*);

- regularly monitor and review all pupils who are on the *Child Protection Register* and/or are the subjects of emergency protection orders, care orders or supervision orders;

- inform all relevant staff of all pupils on the *Child Protection Register*, including the school's education welfare officer;

- pass information to the new school following a change of school, and inform the *Custodian of the Child Protection Register* of the change (the social services department or NSPCC on behalf of the social services department);

- ensure that *all* staff receive training on child protection and on the requirements of the Children Act 1989, including how to report suspicions;

- keep *all* staff informed about child protection issues;

- develop effective links with other agencies and support services.

18 Schools and colleges should recognise the importance of the role played by the Designated Teacher and should enable him or her to carry out the duties of that role effectively and with appropriate training. (DfEE, 1995a, p.6)

In a case of suspected child abuse the Designated Teacher should:

- make sure that all relevant evidence is recorded on the same day; observations, quotes, records of any conversations with the pupil and any other concerned persons. *Note: on no account should any pupil or adult be asked to write a statement themselves*, although it is permissible for the Designated Teacher to make notes of any statements or conversations and to record these in the school's 'Incident book' or 'Day book'.[1] (Proformas for an 'Incident report' or 'Incident needing physical restraint' are given in Figures 5.2 and 5.3, pages 64 and 65);

- inform the social services department or NSPCC of the circumstances – if necessary the emergency duty team (*Note*: the social services department or the NSPCC will inform the police, if necessary);

- send a written report to the social worker who deals with the case as soon as possible. Remember that the pupil's parent(s)/carer(s) may have access to this report in any subsequent child protection conference and/or court proceedings. Reports should include details of:
  - educational progress and achievements;
  - attendance;
  - behaviour;
  - participation in school activities;
  - relations with other children and adults;
  - where relevant, family structure and what is known of the child's position in the family.

  All reports should be based on *evidence*, distinguishing between fact, observations made, reports of conversations, allegations and opinion;

- attend any subsequent *Child Protection Conference* or arrange for a representative to attend. Prior to the conference, a report should be sent for consideration. Make sure that the representative is someone who knows the child well, such as the class teacher or group tutor;

- if a child's name is placed on the *Child Protection Register*, ensure that an appropriate member of staff becomes a member of the *Core Group* and is available to attend all core group meetings.

A *Core Group* is appointed at the *Child Protection Conference* and is responsible for ensuring the implementation of the child's own *Child Protection Plan*; this plan is formulated to ensure that any risk of 'significant harm' (see p.54) to the child is eliminated.

It should be borne in mind that *children with special educational needs* can be especially vulnerable to abuse.

Keeping safe

Just as in situations of bullying (see Chapter 4, Bullying), pupils need to know who they can turn to in confidence if they are concerned about the way in which they are being treated. A 'Worry sheet' (see Figure 5.1), pinned in each teaching space or in the back of each pupil's daily log or homework diary, giving the names and telephone numbers of those who can help, can give them access to appropriate help.

Issues of *keeping safe* can be addressed as part of the school's programme of personal and social development. Details of useful materials may be found at the end of this book.

Worry Sheet

These are people you can talk to or telephone if you are worried or upset about anything which has happened to you, at school or at home:

Fill in the telephone numbers:

Your Parents/Carers _____   Telephone: _____

Your own Social Worker _____   Telephone: _____

The Education Welfare Officer _____   Telephone: _____

Your Group Tutor _____

The Headteacher or Deputy Headteacher _____

The Chair of the Governors _____   Telephone: _____

Childline: **Telephone: 0800 1111**

National Child Protection Line: **Telephone 0800 800 500**

Whatever you say, you will be listened to and what you say will be treated seriously.

Figure 5.1 *Worry sheet*

Protecting adults in schools

Schools have a responsibility to protect their pupils by employing teachers and other workers who are not likely to abuse them. For teachers, they can check List 99:

> List 99 contains the names, dates of birth and teacher reference numbers of people whose employment has been barred or restricted, either on grounds of misconduct or on medical grounds. (DfEE, 1995b, para. 52, p.15)

For all prospective employees, they can check with the police for any criminal background as advised in Circular 9/93 (DfE, 1993b).

Once an adult is employed within a school they need to be able to protect themselves from allegation of abuse and in particular, should:

- be able to develop working practices which minimize the risk of being accused of abusing pupils;

- take the necessary steps to protect themselves from accusations;

- deal with any false allegations which might be made against them.

Care and control

The Children Act 1989 (HMSO, 1989) states that in any legal proceedings, 'the child's welfare shall be the court's paramount consideration' (Masson and Morris, 1992).

Modern society, quite rightly, places great emphasis on the rights of the child and children's allegations of possible assault are listened to very seriously by the caring professions. By the nature of the relationship between adults and pupils in schools, it is sometimes necessary for adults to demonstrate caring by *control*. Sometimes, where pupils are out of control, this means physical control. Staff should at all times be aware of the levels of permissible control and their responsibilities to the pupils they are working with. At the same time, they need to protect themselves.

The government has issued guidelines on permissible forms of 'physical containment' in Circular 9/94 (DfE, 1994c, paras 115–17, pp.37–38). LEAs also have policies on the permissible forms of physical control and restraint and these should be appended to the whole school behaviour policy and formally approved by the governing body as official school policy. Any action which is questioned, consequent to an incident, will then have been undertaken in accordance with official procedures. Should any court action follow, accused members of staff will be more secure.

Adults working with children are only authorized to employ physical restraint where:

- they believe that all other alternatives have failed;
- pupils are at risk of physical injury;
- a pupil's actions are placing other pupils or adults at risk of injury;
- significant damage to property can be limited;
- it does not endanger the physical safety of pupils or staff.

An adult failing to take such action in the interests of the pupil/s in his or her care may be deemed to be negligent in subsequent court proceedings.

In addition, the following guidelines should be followed:

- The level of force must be the *minimum* necessary to ensure the safety of the pupils and adults.
- It is illegal to hit pupils under any circumstances.
- Only approved methods of handling must be used and it is the responsibility of the headteacher to ensure that staff receive regular training.
- A second adult should be involved wherever possible in order to protect the pupils and adults.
- The incident should be reported to the Designated Teacher.
- Any incidents of inappropriate behaviour involving the welfare of pupils and adults, any incidents of violence between pupils and staff, including any incidents of physical restraint and serious damage to property, must be recorded in the establishment's 'Incident book' or 'Day book'.[1]
- In the case of injury to any pupil or adult, notes should be taken in writing, from interviews with each pupil and adult present. *On no account should written statements be taken from pupils or adults.*
- The Designated Teacher should liaise with parents and the social services department, where appropriate.

Schools can protect their staffs by:

- making sure that all staff receive training on child protection issues, including protecting themselves from false allegations;

- having clear guidelines on the physical care and control of pupils, which have been passed as official school policy by the governors. (In schools for children with emotional and behavioural difficulties and in PRUs, training should be given to staff on permitted forms of physical restraint);

- having clear guidelines on procedures for dealing with incidents of child abuse;

- encouraging staff to seek the legal protection of a trade union or professional indemnity insurance;

- supporting accused staff by offering counselling and advice;

- arranging independent counselling for school staff who have an accused colleague, possibly from an independent child welfare consultant;

- appointing a governor with responsibility for child protection.

Adults working in schools can protect themselves by:

- not putting themselves into potentially compromising situations (eg, alone in a changing room with a pupil with the door closed);

- never physically controlling or restraining a pupil alone;

- reporting any injuries sustained in school to the Designated Teacher and making a record in the school's 'Incident book' or 'Day book';[1]

- joining a trade union which has a clear policy on staff protection and which employs specialist legal help if necessary, or by taking out a professional indemnity insurance;

- always taking a 'friend' (for example, a union official) to any meeting where conduct over the handling of a pupil is questioned);

- making detailed, personal notes of the incident, together with any statements from witnesses at the time, and keeping a diary of all information which subsequently comes to light.

When a member of staff is accused of abusing a pupil:

In addition to the information and advice in this chapter, Circular 10/95, *Protecting Children from Abuse* (DfEE, 1995a) should be taken into account; in particular, 'Allegations against staff' (p.11) and the Annex, 'Teachers and child protection', 'Teachers facing allegations of physical/sexual abuse' and 'Guidelines on practice and procedure' (p.15). In general:

- the guidelines given in the annex to Circular 10/95 on procedures for dealing with allegations against staff should be adhered to at all time;

- it is the responsibility of the headteacher (the governors, in the case of an accused headteacher) to decide whether or not to suspend the accused person and the prime consideration must be the continuing safety of the pupils.

  Although such suspensions are 'without prejudice', any suspension is seen by the pupils, parents/carers and the general public at large as implying guilt. Consequently, suspensions should be avoided wherever possible.

The head teacher or governors will need to take into account the seriousness and plausibility of the allegation, the risk of harm to the pupil concerned or to other pupils, and the possibilities of tampering with evidence, as well as the interests of the person concerned and the school.   (DfEE, 1995a, para 48, p.11)

- the full evidence should be made available to the accused person without delay;

- the pupil in question should not be allowed contact with the accused person or with any potential witnesses, where an allegation is made by a pupil or parent;

- if the allegation is made by another member of staff, the person making the allegation should not be allowed to continue working with that pupil, his or her parents/carers, or with potential witnesses, while investigations are proceeding;

- if the allegation is made by another member of staff, and the allegation is found to be malicious, that person should be disciplined;

- the accused person and the whole school staff should have access to supportive counselling services, possibly from an independent child welfare consultant;

- the member of the school's governing body with responsibility for child protection should keep in touch with accused members of staff.

Written records

The following *must* be noted in the school's 'Incident book' or 'Day book':[1]

- any inappropriate behaviour which involves physical contact and/or injury between pupils or staff;

- any serious damage to property;

- any physical restraint used.

Written statements must not be taken from pupils or adults, although detailed notes should be made of any interviews.[1] The accounts must include:

- the time and place of the incident;
- the *antecedents* of the incident;
- details of *exactly* what happened;
- the *consequences* of the incident, including a note of all injuries sustained by staff and/or pupils;
- in the case of serious injury and/or damage to property, the names of all witnesses and notes of any interviews with witnesses.

Proformas for reporting incidents and physical restraint are shown on pages 64 and 65.

A separate policy for child and adult protection?

All of the above could form the basis for a separate policy for child and adult protection or could be incorporated into the whole-school behaviour policy. Whichever approach is chosen, the policy for child protection must be compatible with the values and ethos underpinning the whole-school behaviour policy.

NOTE
1. Schools organize their record-keeping in different ways. In large schools these might be kept in years or departments, in small schools for the whole school. However the records are kept, all schools are obliged to keep records of serious incidents of abuse, injuries to staff or pupils and serious damage to property.

   These records must be made available for inspection by the governors, senior officials of the local authority or OFSTED inspectors, on request.

INCIDENT REPORT FORM

Name of person completing this form: _____

Location of incident: _____ Date: _____ Time: _____

Other forms completed: Physical restraint ☐   Accident: Pupil ☐   Accident: Adult ☐

Pupil(s) involved:

Staff involved:

Summary of incident:

Any sanctions/punishments already given:

Further action necessary:	By whom:

Signed: _____ Date: _____

Figure 5.2 *Incident report form*

PHYSICAL RESTRAINT REPORT FORM

Name of pupil: _____ Date: _____ Time: _____

Location of incident: _____ Length of incident: _____

Activity: _____

Restraint used: ✓

Holding one hand, adult facing pupil	
Holding one wrist, adult facing pupil	
Holding two hands, adult facing pupil	
Holding two wrists, adult facing pupil	
Holding hands or wrists, adult behind pupil	
Arms crossed, adult's arms round pupil, adult behind pupil	
Adult's arms and legs wrapped round pupil, adult behind pupil	
Pupil sitting on chair	
Pupil sitting on floor	
Pupil lying on floor, face up	
Pupil lying on floor, face down	

Signed (Member of staff restraining child): _____

Signed (Staff witness) _____

Action taken by member of Senior Management Team on call ✓ ✗ N/A

Incident discussed with staff involved	
Incident discussed with all staff	
Pupil interviewed	
Parents/carers informed/involved in discussion	
Pupil's social worker informed	
Other workers informed (specify)	
Further action necessary (specify) – and by whom:	

Signed: _____ Position: _____ Date: _____

Figure 5.3 *Physical restraint report form*

Chapter 6

Equal opportunities

Access to the curriculum and behaviour

As far as behaviour is concerned, it is useful to look at equal opportunities in terms of how behaviour can affect access to the curriculum.

> All pupils share the right to a broad and balanced curriculum, including the National Curriculum.　　　　　　　　　　　　　　　　　　(NCC, 1989)

OFSTED inspectors judge what pupils *know, understand and can do* in relation to their age and ability levels.

'Curriculum entitlement' is a difficult concept to define and it might be helpful to examine it in general terms. The following is a development of ideas taken from the HMI booklet, *The Curriculum from 5–16* (DES, 1989b):

Curriculum entitlement should relate to an individual's needs in the areas of *knowledge, experiences* and *skills*. The following elements should meet the needs of any child:

1. A statement of aims for the education of that individual in relation to his or her needs within the community, now and in the future
   - in relation to human value
   - in relation to individual uniqueness
   - in relation to the family
   - in relation to becoming a citizen
   - in relation to appreciating learning for itself.

2. A statement of learning for the individual's development of skills, attitudes, experiences and knowledge
   - personal growth
   - emotional growth

- the acquisition of skills relevant to the individual's needs:
  - communication
  - observation
  - study
  - problem solving
  - physical and practical
  - creative and imaginative
  - numerical
  - personal and social
- the ability to relate positively to others.

3. A balanced programme of learning experiences within each learning objective
   - to ensure relevance for each individual
   - differentiated according to need
   - progression according to need
   - to encourage effective communication through a variety of media
   - to encourage creativity and self-expression
   - to understand experiences:
     - aesthetic and creative
     - human and social
     - linguistic and literary
     - mathematical
     - moral
     - physical
     - scientific
     - spiritual
     - technological
   - to encourage an understanding of self and human values
     - reliability
     - initiative
     - self-discipline
     - tolerance
     - self-confidence
     - adaptability
     - perseverance
     - sensitivity
   - to understand the structure and function of:
     - objects
     - systems
     - processes.

4. Staffing and resource allocation based on the principle of equality of curricular opportunity
   - identification of the needs of particular individuals and groups
   - effective deployment of resources
   - balance between the needs of pupils, teachers and resources.

5. Effective skills in teaching which promote the process of individual learning
   - a variety of teaching techniques including:
     - objectives setting and planning
     - the chance to experience success in learning
     - experiential learning
     - investigation
     - application of skills and knowledge
     - opportunity for reflection
     - positive feedback
     - progressive learning
     - cooperation and sharing
     - group work
     - negotiation
     - ongoing review
     - being valued.

6. Participative, effective assessment
   - to monitor the learning experiences
   - to help set the personal goals of the learner
   - to set teaching objectives
   - to provide an opportunity for positive feedback
   - to assess the need for guidance and counselling.

7. Evaluation
   - between colleagues
   - between pupils
   - pupil/teacher
   - against external criteria.

Sometimes, children who exhibit behavioural difficulties affect the learning of others. They are often removed from the teaching group or even excluded from the school. In such cases, access to the whole curriculum is denied, raising questions about equality of opportunity for the pupils who are excluded. *Attention should be paid to the curricular needs of withdrawn or excluded pupils*, at the same time as paying attention to the effects on teaching and learning if disruptive pupils remain in the group or in the school.

Often, children who exhibit inappropriate behaviour have associated learning difficulties. There is, therefore, a tendency to place them in teaching groups which relate to their achievements, rather than to their ability. This can have a negative effect on the children's self-esteem and provoke ongoing inappropriate behaviour.

Sometimes it is difficult to assess when such children have achieved in learning, as they have little to show for their efforts on paper. However, alternative methods of assessment, for example orally or using Information Technology, can demonstrate that knowledge has been retained and skills learnt. (See page 27 for more information about the ways in which the curriculum can be differentiated for pupils with behavioural difficulties.)

A whole-school behaviour policy needs to consider the equal opportunities issues over access to the entitlement curriculum.

Gender and behaviour

The National Exclusions Reporting System figures on school exclusions (DfE, 1993a) show that exclusions are 4:1, boys to girls in 1990/91 and 5:1, boys to girls in 1991/92. Separate figures for the numbers of boys and girls given statements of special educational need for emotional and behavioural difficulties are not available according to a DfEE spokesperson.

These figures reinforce what most teachers would confirm, that boys present far more overt behavioural difficulties than girls and consequently tend to end up being punished or excluded from teaching more frequently than girls. This has considerable implications for equality of opportunity and needs to be taken into account in any whole-school behaviour policy. (See also Chapter 3, Rewards and sanctions).

Race and behaviour

Children who feel that their racial and cultural backgrounds are not taken seriously or are not valued, are more likely to exhibit antisocial inappropriate behaviour. Access to cultural events, and an opportunity to take part in festivals and celebrations relating to cultural backgrounds and religions, are important facets of ensuring a positive school ethos. However, Grimshaw (1994) in the National Children's Bureau's survey of residential provision for children with emotional and behavioural difficulties found that 'Children from minority ethnic groups did not appear to show particular patterns of opposition or conformity' (p.80).

Nevertheless, Cooper *et al.* (1991) found that there are disproportionate numbers of children from some minority ethnic groups in schools for children with emotional and behavioural difficulties. Of these, most were of mixed parentage or of African-Caribbean groups. This could mean that these children's inappropriate behaviour was a reaction against discrimination, which has implications for any school's policy and practice on equal opportunities and for the whole-school behaviour policy.

Adults working in schools also need to be sensitive to culture-specific behaviour in order not to label it 'inappropriate'.

Chapter 7

Involving parents

Parents or carers?

It is embarrassing and sometimes hurtful to a child if the teacher refers to a particular parent who, perhaps, is not actually living with the child, or may even be dead. All the points made with regard to parents in this chapter apply equally to carers.

It is important to use the child's own names for the adults at home when talking to them – 'What did Mum say?', 'What did Fred [Mum's partner] say?'

Adults in schools who have a lot of contact with a particular child should make sure that they know:

- What the home circumstances are. Does the child live with parents, step-parents or with a foster parent? Who is the child's primary carer?

- Who has *parental responsibility* under The Children Act 1989 (see below).

- Who has the right to see the child in school.

- Who is legally responsible for making decisions about the child's education.

- Who should be contacted in an emergency and where they can be found.

- Who should be sent copies of letters, reports, invitations, etc.

All these facts should be noted in an easily accessible place in the children's files.

Parental responsibility

> Defined as 'all the rights, duties, powers, responsibilities and authority which by law a parent of a child has in relation to the child and his property' [S3(1)].

> Parental responsibility can be exercised by persons who are not the child's biological parent and can be shared among a number of persons. It can be acquired by agreement or court order.   (Home Office *et al.*, 1991, p.123)

This means, for example, that, although the birth mother automatically has parental responsibility for her child, the father of a child does not automatically have parental responsibility unless: (a) he is married to the child's mother at the time of the child's birth, or (b) he has been granted responsibility by the courts, or (c) he has entered into a parental responsibility agreement with the mother.

Why involve parents/carers?

> Parents are the first educators. They play a crucial part in shaping their children's personalities and attitudes. They continue to have a powerful influence over them throughout their school years.   (DES, 1989a, para. 1, p.133)

One of the important conclusions of the research leading to *School Matters* (Mortimore *et al.*, 1988) was that the most effective junior schools are those which have the best informal contacts with parents. However, despite all the exhortations that teachers should promote better relationships between schools and home, some teachers remain very suspicious of parents/carers, and some parents/carers do not feel comfortable about talking to teachers.

Many teachers blame parents/carers for their children's misbehaviour in school. However, while there may be a small number of parents/carers who are actively hostile to schools, 'the vast majority of parents, regardless of social class, ethnic or cultural origin, want their children to work hard and behave well at school' (DES, 1989a, p.125). Parents/carers are, potentially, crucial allies in working with a child's inappropriate behaviour and no advantage can be gained from making them feel guilty or hostile towards the school. However, if they only receive negative feedback from schools it is small wonder that they develop hostile feelings towards them.

Parents/carers usually want to cooperate with schools over the behaviour of their children. However, they sometimes find great difficulty in understanding the expectations of the schools.

> [Headteachers] should ensure that their school behaviour policies are communicated fully and clearly to parents, who should be reminded of them regularly and informed of any major changes to them throughout their child's school career.   (DES, 1989a, R.64, p.129)

Often children behave inappropriately at school because of factors at home and yet, at the same time, schools often involve parents/carers in resolving behaviour problems as a last resort; 'Headteachers and teachers should involve parents at an early stage rather than as a last resort' (DES, 1989a, R.58, p.126).

Parents/carers sometimes tell teachers that their child behaves appropriately at home. Although teachers tend to disbelieve this, it is usually true, and 'They should take that into account when discussing pupils with their parents' (DES, 1989a, R.59, p.126).

Children respond to the involvement of parents/carers in any system of rewards and punishments. In a survey of secondary pupils, Wheldall and Merritt (1988) found that a positive letter home was one of the two most valued rewards. Pupils dislike letters home to parents/carers or being put on report as a response to inappropriate behaviour, and such a response is likely to provoke disaffection. Wheldall and Merritt (1988) point out that, while letters of complaint are often written to parents, letters of praise are rarely sent. *(Note:* the comments on letters to parents/carers on page 44.)

> We recommend that headteachers and teachers should ensure that parents receive positive constructive comments on their children's work and behaviour as a matter of course. (DES, 1989a, R.57, p.125)

Areas for parental/carer involvement

(Some of these suggestions are more appropriate to primary and special schools.)

Externally:
- follow-up school work at home
- help in setting and reviewing targets for achievement in learning
- help in setting and reviewing targets for achievement in behaviour
- fund-raising
- taking part in school functions
- donating materials/time
- parent governors.

Internally:
- help within the classroom – basic chores
- help to support pupils with difficulties in basic skills
- listen to good readers
- give attention, praise and encouragement to certain pupils
- organize facilities for other parents
- drop into the school for a cup of coffee
- help with school functions
- help with school journeys.

Parents/carers are likely to be more effectively involved within the school if they:

- understand the way in which the school organizes the management of learning
- understand the way in which behaviour is managed
- know who is 'in charge' and who to refer to for help
- are given specific tasks.

Note. It should be made clear to any parents/carers who help in schools that they are there as helpers and not teachers. No amount of help or support in the classroom can make up for the skills of the professional teacher. They must clearly understand that they are there to assist the children to learn under the direction of the class teacher. The teaching unions have clear and useful advice on the use of helpers in classrooms.

Meetings with parents/carers

Often, teachers only meet parents/carers when there is something to be put right. If parents/carers do not feel at ease, or feel that they have been 'sent for', they will resent the meeting and are unlikely to cooperate with the school in this process. No matter what the meeting is for, it can be made much more positive if:

- parents/carers know the reason for the meeting in advance

- the invitation is made in person or over the telephone. It often helps to confirm in writing (parents have been known to forget meetings!)

- invitations to the meeting are couched in positive and welcoming terms

- the time of the meeting fits in with the family's commitments

- the parent/carer is invited to bring a friend, relative or social worker to the meeting with them

- there is an interpreter present, if necessary

- other key members of the school community are involved

- all the information necessary for the meeting is to hand

- there is a suitable, comfortable room available with facilities for looking after any other children who might be brought into the meeting and for making refreshments

- the greetings are friendly and informal, using names

- an interest is expressed in the family as a whole

- it is demonstrated that the child is valued

- the subject for discussion is explained to the parents/carers and they are asked if there is anything they want to raise during the meeting.

- it is established what the school and the parents/carers want to achieve from the meeting

- the meeting starts with comments about the child in positive terms and in as non-judgmental a manner as possible.

- the problem – if that is the subject of the meeting – is explained in as positive a manner as possible, and the parents'/carers' opinions about possible solutions are asked from time to time

- a check is made now and again that the parents'/carers' perception of what has been discussed matches the school's

- what has been decided is summarized at the end and it is checked that the parents/carers agree

- the parents/carers are asked if there is anything else which needs to be covered

- the parents/carers and school agree targets for further action, including a further meeting if necessary.

In addition, where there is a dispute between parents/carers and the school over the handling of their child, it can help to have an independent chair for the meeting who is able to meet with the parents/carers before the meeting.

Of course, such a list is far too long for day-to-day use but it can be used as a checklist for any meetings which are set up. In general, schools should try to ensure that parents/carers are:

- approached in a sensitive manner

- made to feel part of the process of defining any problem and seeking solutions

- made to feel at home in the school

- in agreement with and understand what has been decided.

After the meeting:

- a brief report should be written and, if a problem was discussed, details should be included on what the problem was, what was agreed should be done about it and the targets for those involved

- it should be checked that the child agrees with the report and it should be altered, if necessary

- a copy should be sent to the parents/carers for their comments and it should be altered in the light of these, if necessary.

Reporting to parents/carers

Schools have to provide regular reports to parents/carers about progress in learning and in behaviour. It was suggested in Chapter 3, Rewards and sanctions, that schools should communicate with parents/carers regularly in order to reinforce progress in learning and in behaviour. In general, reports to parents/carers should:

- concentrate on small target steps
- avoid general comments like, 'He's been good today'
- describe actual appropriate behaviour related to the pupil's targets: 'She has stayed in her seat all day', for instance
- leave a space for the parents' own comments and so they can give examples of appropriate behaviour at home
- be regular (if possible, daily)
- be discussed with the child (and read to him or her, if necessary) before it is sent to the parents/carers.

Communications from parents/carers should be:

- made known to all appropriate staff
- filed carefully and referenced in the school's 'Day book' or whatever form of recording the school has adopted for written communications
- noted in the school's 'Day book' or whatever form of recording the school has adopted for verbal communications and 'phone calls.

Report cards with a standard format like the example in Figure 7.1 (which is more appropriate for primary and some special schools), based on a behaviour target, or a home/school book, can be an effective way of keeping parents/carers informed and involved.

☺ **Good news!**

for _____ from _____ School

☹ As you know we have all been concerned about:

_____

☺ _____ (name of pupil) agreed

_____

☺ You _____ (name of parent/carer) agreed

_____

☺ The school agreed

_____

Today _____ has managed to

_____

_____

_____

We know you will want to join us in saying

☺ **well done!** ☺

Figure 7.1 *Sample report card*

Chapter 8

Support for all

Support for children with emotional and behavioural difficulties

More and more pupils with emotional and behavioural difficulties (EBD) are remaining in mainstream schools, not least because the process of assessment is so lengthy, and all teachers need to know something about good practice in supporting them. (See also the section on differentiation and emotional and behavioural difficulties, page 27.)

It could be argued that the effective teacher is one who enables pupils to realize their full academic potential and to succeed in learning. However teachers of pupils with emotional and behavioural difficulties recognize that such pupils must be enabled to come to terms with, and deal with, their underlying personal and social difficulties before teaching and learning can occur and this needs to underpin any whole-school behaviour policy.

Within the framework of a person's personality and the experiences which have formed his or her self-esteem, behaviour is always logical, if unacceptable:

> ...even though we do not have the wisdom to enumerate the behaviour of another person, we can grant that every individual does have his own private world of meaning, conceived out of the integrity of his personality.
>
> (Axline, 1966, p.15)

Teachers need qualities of maturity, warmth, insight and a sense of humour to be able to have insight into the emotional needs of their pupils. Wilson (1985, p.82) defined the attributes of what she described as the 'good' teacher in these terms:

The good teacher shows a caring attitude, courtesy, respect, humanity, kindness and interest. These are conveyed by the way one speaks to the children and comments on their work. I have asked children who had had problems why they were doing better now, and they would say: 'The teachers here care about you, they mind about you, they listen to you' or 'They don't shout at you and make you feel silly'.

She stressed the importance of the child feeling that he or she can '...talk things over with a teacher'..., '... there is a way of listening which any human being can do'. This might well be so, but some people have to work at it!

Rogers (1969) examined the characteristics of the successful counsellor and said that they need *acceptance, genuineness* and *empathy*. *Acceptance* means unconditionally accepting the child as a person, without condoning or accepting the behaviour being exhibited. *Genuineness* means that the child must feel that the person is sincere. *Empathy* is the concept of putting oneself into the place of the child and appreciating his or her feelings and concerns while not moving from one's own place:

> To sense the client's private world as if it were your own, but without ever losing the 'as if' quality – this is empathy, and this seems essential to therapy.
>
> (Rogers, 1967)

Rogers (1969, pp.164–5) lists ten guidelines for creating a facilitating emotional and intellectual ethos:

1 The teacher must communicate his [sic] trust in the student from the very start.
2 He [sic] must help students to clarify and articulate their individual group objectives.
3 He must assume that pupils have intrinsic motivation that will enable them to pursue their studies.
4 He must act as a resource person who makes available the widest range of learning experiences possible for the objectives selected.
5 He should be a resource person for each individual.
6 He should learn to recognise and accept emotional messages expressed within the group.
7 He should be an active participant in the group.
8 He should maintain empathetic understanding of group members' feelings.
9 Finally, he must know himself.

A child's self-esteem, as discussed in Chapter 2, Teaching and learning, is influenced by the information he or she receives back from 'significant others'. The teacher is an important *significant other* to his or her pupils and therefore needs to be able to provide conditions for teaching and learning which enable the pupils to succeed and to make favourable judgements about themselves.

> Among the conditions that appear to be associated with the development of positive self-judgement are acceptance, clearly defined limits, respectful treatment, reasonable yet challenging standards and psychological defences to deal with adversity.   (Coopersmith and Feldman, 1974, p.203)

At the same time:

> ...children need guidelines within which to operate, standards to gauge competence and progress, and assistance in dealing with difficulties beyond their immediate present skills.   (*ibid.*)

For older children, the members of the peer group form 'significant others'. For this reason, a system of positive behaviour management (see Chapter 9, The difficult pupil), based on group responsibility can prove effective. The child needs:

- to feel that 'significant others' care about him or her,
- standards to use as guidelines for progress,
- stable and secure boundaries within which he or she can feel secure.

Children do not come into this world with their own framework of controls; they need to have a secure *external* framework of control until they develop their own *internal* personal controls.

Any demonstration of what is perceived by a child as adult 'weakness' will result in insecurity and consequent acting out; testing to see how secure the situation is. Often, teachers have to make their pupils feel secure by demonstrating their control in a manner which is larger than life. As has already been discussed in Chapter 5, Pupil and staff protection, *the teacher demonstrates caring by controlling.*

Following The Children Act 1989 (HMSO, 1989) and the greater attention being given to children's 'rights', teachers are becoming reluctant to demonstrate care and control over their pupils. There is a very fine dividing line between care and control on the one hand and assault on the other. Adults working with pupils in schools must be careful to ensure that they operate within the school's, LEA's and government guidelines at all times (see Chapter 5, Pupil and staff protection).

Support for teachers

Teaching is a very individual skill. As effective headteachers know, every teacher on their staff teaches in a completely different way, in accordance with their own personality. At the centre of each individual teacher's approach is the way in which he or she relates to others, and in particular, to the pupils. This depends on the way in which the teacher feels about him or herself. Teachers are more likely to feel secure and to be effective if they feel liked and respected by the pupils they teach. Teachers are most likely to feel insecure and inadequate when challenged by their pupils' inappropriate behaviour and they are less likely to feel like this if they feel supported by the school's whole-school behaviour policy and by the Senior Management Team.

The self-confidence of the teacher in his or her own skills is also important. It seems as if a teacher can make any approach work, simply because he or she believes that it *will* work and this provides the security within which the pupils can learn. This was clearly demonstrated by the National Foundation for Educational Research investigation into different teaching styles (Barker-Lunn, 1984). Both 'formal' and 'informal' teaching styles were found to be effective and the research team suggested that it is the teacher's belief and confidence in the approach which he or she uses which makes it effective.

The self-esteem of teachers

The personality and self-esteem of the individual teacher seems to be an important factor in teacher effectiveness. Self theory indicates that teachers who have a clear and positive sense of self, together with confidence in their professional abilities, are most likely to enhance the self-esteem of their pupils and hence their motivation to learn. Pupils value teachers who they perceive as warm and understanding, but at the same time, not a 'soft touch'.

Combs (in Hamachek, 1978, p.167) cites several studies which indicate the way in which good teachers typically see themselves:

1. Good teachers see themselves as identified with people rather than withdrawn, removed, apart from or alienated from others.
2. Good teachers feel basically adequate rather than inadequate. They do not see themselves as generally unable to cope with problems.
3. Good teachers feel trustworthy rather than untrustworthy. They see themselves as reliable, dependable individuals, with the potential for coping with events as they happen.
4. Good teachers see themselves as wanted rather than unwanted. They see themselves as likeable and attractive (in a personal not physical sense), as opposed to feeling ignored and rejected.
5. Good teachers see themselves as worthy rather than unworthy. They see themselves as people of consequence, dignity and integrity as opposed to feeling they matter little, can be overlooked and discounted.

'Good' workers in any sphere probably feel in this way about themselves but it is because of its effect on the pupils that teachers' own self-esteem is of such importance.

Teachers with low self-esteem are more likely to take inappropriate behaviour as aimed at them personally and they are certainly not going to be able to enhance a pupil's low self-esteem through the teaching and learning process if they feel threatened when a pupil rejects their teaching. They tend to get into confrontations in a 'no-win' situation and to raise their own self-esteem at the cost of others'. Trust has to be earned and cannot be imposed by over-authoritarian didactic approaches. (See the discussion on 'deviance provocative' and 'deviance insulative' teachers in Chapter 2, Teaching and learning, page 22.)

In one of the few pieces of research into self-esteem and the effectiveness of teachers working with children with emotional and behavioural difficulties, Scheuer (1971) found that there was a significant gain in academic achievement in children who saw their teachers as possessing a high degree of unconditional regard for them.

Reflecting on practice and 'supervision'

Schön (1983) has developed the concept of the professional who adopts a strategy of 'reflection-in-action'. He maintains that 'professional practice has at least as much to do with finding the problem as with solving the problem found'. Reflection-in-action is a process of thinking on one's feet.

The 'professional' is a person who comes across the same occurrences in his or her work again and again and is able to use the experiences gained to deal with new experiences – a system of what Schön calls 'knowing-in-action'. Such use of the skills acquired by experience has a positive effect on the professional's self-esteem. However, 'If the professional learns to be selectively inattentive to phenomena that do not fit the categories of his knowing-in-action, then he may suffer boredom or "burnout"'.

Schön (1983, p.330) draws a firm distinction between the 'expert' and the 'reflective practitioner', as shown in Table 8.1. He sees the professional development of the teacher as based on a system of 'supervision' which 'would concern itself less with maintaining the teacher's coverage of curriculum content than with assessment and support of the teacher's reflection-in-action'.

Table 8.1 *Schön's 'expert' and 'reflective practitioner'*

Expert	Reflective practitioner
I am presumed to know and must claim to do so regardless of my own uncertainty...	I am presumed to know, but I am not the only one in the situation to have relevant and important knowledge. My uncertainties may be a source of learning for me and for them...

Keep my distance from the client and hold on to the expert's role. Give the client a sense of my expertise but convey a feeling of warmth and sympathy as a 'sweetener'...	Seek out connections to the client's thoughts and feelings. Allow his respect for my knowledge to emerge from his discovery of it in the situation...
Look for deference and status in the client's response to my professional persona	Look for the sense of freedom and of real connection to the client as a consequence of no longer needing to maintain a professional facade

What use is the National Curriculum (DfE, 1995) to pupils or teachers if teachers only feel secure in their subject area and do not feel secure in their own personalities and professional skills? Teaching is, above all, a *relationship* between teacher and pupil.

Supervision

The social work profession has support and professional reflection and development built into its system of 'supervision'. In this model, each social worker has a regular session with his or her senior in which they both reflect on concerns over practice and the senior makes the worker aware of skills and personal strengths which he or she has used on previous occasions. They then discuss how these skills and strengths can be used to overcome new concerns as they arise. This model seems very suitable for schools, presupposing that it is non-judgmental.

Easen (1985, p.129) links this kind of process into a whole-school approach by introducing the concept of 'thinking schools':

...'thinking' schools begin with 'reflecting' teachers; teachers who establish for themselves what are their 'limits' and how they can reach beyond them; teachers who establish an inner dialogue between the action they take and the reflection they make; teachers who establish their own 'vision' for their own practice.

Easen points out that much of the process of 'coming to take charge of your own world and, in particular, of having real control over your own learning' is to do with confidence: 'Confidence both to define and resolve one's own problems' ... 'Needs have to be defined both in terms of immediate awareness and of understanding the cultural and psychological assumptions influencing the perception of needs'. He says that 'if a school wishes to draw upon external agencies, it should be in order to service those teachers who have realized their own power and wish to create change for themselves'. However, he goes on to point out that teachers, like everyone else, tend to cling to their self-image: 'the urge to maintain a consistent self-image is so strong that we tend to deny, ignore or manipulate evidence to eliminate contradictions'.

Such an approach, built into the whole-school behaviour policy could be used to facilitate:

- reflection on success in teaching for each teacher,

- the use of the knowledge of their success in solving difficulties in areas of concern,

- enabling them to feel better teachers and increase their self-esteem.

Appraisal

The recommendations of the National Steering Group on teacher appraisal (DES, 1989c, p.3) are compatible with this approach. It sees the aims of appraisal as being:

> ...a continuous and systematic process intended to help individual teachers with their professional development and career planning, and to help ensure that the in-service training and deployment of teachers matches the complementary needs of individual teachers and schools.

It advocates that appraisal should start with 'self-appraisal': that all teachers should be expected to reflect on their own performance.

At the core of teacher appraisal would be the 'Appraisal interview', which should involve:

- further consideration, if necessary, of the teacher's job description
- review of the work done, successes and areas for development identified since the last appraisal
- discussion of professional development needs
- discussion of career development, as appropriate
- discussion of the appraisee's role in, and contribution to, the policies and management of the school, and any constraints placed on the appraisee's work by the school context
- identification of targets for future action/development
- clarification of points to be included in the appraisal statement.   (p.11)

It notes that appraisal interviews are likely to be successful only when:

- both appraiser and appraisee are well informed and well prepared
- the topics to be discussed are agreed in advance
- discussion concentrates on the areas on which information gathering had focused
- the interview is free from interruptions.   (p.12)

The regulations for the appraisal in operation at present, which developed from these proposals, are laid out in Circular 12/91 (DES, 1991). Although one of the aims of appraisal is laid down as 'assisting school teachers to realise their potential' (para. 4), the system in operation is much more geared to dealing with teachers' problems than to encouraging reflection on success. The emphasis is on:

improving skills and performance
identify potential for career development
helping school teachers having difficulties with their performance.

(para. 4).

The proactive emphasis of the Steering Group has been replaced with a more reactive emphasis in the regulations. Nevertheless, schools have considerable latitude over their interpretation of the regulations.

Professional development

The work of schools with pupils who exhibit inappropriate behaviour can be much more effective if at least one member of staff moves on one step from the school's positive system of personal reflection, supervision and appraisal to specific training in working with pupils who exhibit the ultimate in inappropriate behaviour: those with emotional and behavioural difficulties.

Unfortunately, most of the current training available takes place under the special educational needs (SEN) umbrella. This means that teachers undertaking a 'generic' SEN training receive training in dealing with pupils' learning difficulties but little or no help in dealing with their personal, social or behavioural difficulties, particularly over the practical management of behaviour and in organizing the curriculum in the way which has been described in Chapter 2, Teaching and learning, page 29. While training in working with pupils with learning difficulties can assist teachers to develop frameworks for identification, target-setting and assessment of special educational needs in general, they are ill-prepared, personally and professionally, for working with these pupils.

It is debatable if behaviour problems fit easily into the learning difficulties model of SEN. For most pupils with special educational needs, the difficulties either relate to access to the learning facilities and special equipment to facilitate learning, or to organizing the *content* of the curriculum differently. Pupils who exhibit inappropriate behaviour may well have learning difficulties, but these cannot be resolved unless attention is paid to their personal and social difficulties and often, teaching and learning cannot take place until then. It is the *process* element of teaching and learning within the curriculum which needs to be addressed (see Chapter 2, Teaching and learning).

Training courses need to recognize the importance of personal reflection. Teachers who understand themselves and how they feel about themselves and their life experiences, are better equipped to understand the pupils with whom they are working and also have a greater insight and resilience in their work with pupils who exhibit inappropriate behaviour.

Courses should also pay attention to the effects of personal and social difficulties on learning and the way in which the curriculum can be differentiated (for definitions, see page 27). This differentiation should enable learning experiences to be perceived as relevant by the pupils. This will help to raise their self-esteem through success in learning and in behaviour which will in turn, have a motivating effect.

A fundamental aspect of courses should be a chance to talk to skilled practitioners in a variety of educational settings; what better place to observe emotional growth than in a nursery school, for example? People learn by doing, and modern courses have far too great an emphasis on academic study. Teachers want to know what to do, who should do it, how it should be done and when it should be done. They also want to anticipate any snags they are likely to meet and strategies for dealing with them if they do arise. This is best learned by working alongside and observing skilled workers. Academic lectures have their place, but they are for enabling workers to develop a philosophical background, framework and understanding of the work, not for acquiring personal and professional strength and skills.

Above all, the courses need to give the participants the confidence to believe that they know what to do in organizing the process of teaching and learning and how to exercise appropriate care and control without thinking about it. Such self-confidence will lead to a greater sense of professionalism in the teachers and a sense of security amongst the pupils they teach, leading to a rise in their own self-esteem.

For details of courses which have many of these characteristics, see Appendix III.

Chapter 9

The difficult pupil

How to refer to these pupils is a problem: they are the pupils who, no matter how interesting the work and how stimulating the teaching, still manage to behave inappropriately. They are probably well into the Stage 4 assessment of the *Code of Practice on the Identification and Assessment of Special Educational Needs* (DfE, 1994b) and destined for Stage 5, because of their behavioural or emotional and behavioural difficulties.

This chapter is the last one in this section, quite deliberately, because if the issues discussed in Chapters 1 to 8 have been incorporated into the school's policies and procedures, then there are very few pupils who are not motivated to engage in learning and who do not feel supported and secure within an effective system of positive behaviour management. This chapter is about what to do with these very few children, assuming that there is a fully operational whole-school behaviour policy, within the classroom and around the school.

There must be shared consistent approaches throughout the school, which are accepted and practised by all adults within the school community, and which are based on shared values and positive beliefs about children and the way in which they learn and behave.

Often, the 'difficult pupil' has had unfortunate experiences of failure in learning and in personal relationships which they bring with them into school, and much of the inappropriate behaviour and disaffection which occurs in schools is related to avoiding further pain (see Chapter 2, Teaching and learning). Pupils' learning can be helped by the development of a teacher/pupil relationship which demonstrates that they are valued and that the teacher is interested in them as persons. This relationship can be fostered by:

- greeting the pupils by name at the beginning of the day or session, asking how they are and listening to their 'news'

- giving them special tasks with responsibilities attached
- chatting to the pupils in the corridor, in the playground or at the dinner table
- taking an interest in their achievements and praising them, where appropriate
- a hand on the shoulder (but note the advice in Chapter 5, Pupil and staff protection, on how adults in schools need to protect themselves)
- arranging activities after school
- saying 'goodnight' and implying that tomorrow is a fresh day, when we all start again with a fresh sheet.

This is especially difficult in large schools, where pupils encounter many different teachers in the course of a week, but the principles remain valid at every phase.

Positive behaviour management

One of the most effective ways of working with inappropriate behaviour is by a process of *positive behaviour management*. There are six stages in this process:

1. Describe the behaviour to the pupil – 'this is what you are doing'.

2. Explain why the behaviour is inappropriate by *describing its effects* – 'this is how it is affecting:
   - the group,
   - me,
   - the learning'.

3. Specify the behaviour which would be appropriate:
   - 'this is the way the group as a whole is expected to behave'
   - 'this is how you are expected to behave'.

4. Discuss with the pupil how he/she should be behaving – 'this is how we think you should be behaving in this group'.

5. Discuss achievable, staged targets for the appropriate behaviour with the pupil:
   - 'this is how we expect you to do it
   - in these stages
   - in this period of time'.

6. Review at the end of each session and reiterate or modify the targets for the next session.

Where pupils' behaviour is naughty, as opposed to inappropriate, then the school's system of rewards and sanctions will come into play (see Chapter 3, Rewards and sanctions). It is sometimes difficult to decide when a pupil is being naughty and then discussions with colleagues about their experiences with the pupil in question are very useful. Above all however,

- treat each incident as complete in itself,
- deal with it as soon as possible,
- start each new school day and each new session with a clean sheet.

Defining the nature and frequency of inappropriate behaviour

Teachers sometimes find difficulty in defining inappropriate behaviour in positive terms and using a chart like the one shown in Table 9.1 might help by breaking behaviour into three components, A, B and C:

Antecedents
- What was the activity in progress at the time?
- Was there anything before the incident which might have provoked it?

Behaviour
- What actually happened?
- Who was involved?
- What did the rest of the group do?
- Did anything appear to make it worse?
- What stopped it?

Consequences
- Why did the pupil need to behave in this way?
- What did the pupil get out of it? (What was the 'pay-off'?)
- How did it affect the rest of the group?
- Are the consequences likely to make the inappropriate behaviour recur?

Table 9.1 *A chart for use in defining inappropriate behaviour*

Antecedents – Behaviour – Consequences			
Session, date and time	Antecedents	Behaviour	Consequences

The nature and frequency of appropriate and inappropriate behaviour can be gauged by using the checklists 'Appropriate behaviours' and 'Inappropriate behaviours' (Figures 12.4 and 12.5 on pages 112 and 113) at the end of Chapter 12, Reviewing the operation of the current behaviour policy.

Appropriate and inappropriate behaviour need to be defined before their frequency is observed and recorded. It might be better if a colleague is asked to do this, particularly when the teacher concerned feels that it is something personal.

The observations can be recorded as follows:

- Count the incidents within a set period of time (this can give a comparative figure of so many incidents per hour which can be used for assessing the effectiveness of any strategies which might be undertaken).

- Time the incidents.

- Count the number of times the pupil behaves inappropriately, within the number of times it was possible to behave appropriately. This can be expressed as a percentage.

- Check for inappropriate behaviour over set periods of time (every 10 minutes, for example) and record a tick (✓) or a cross (✗) for each incident.

Targets for strategies can be set for reinforcing appropriate behaviour and discouraging inappropriate behaviour after observing the frequency. The observations can be repeated after a set period of time in order to assess the effectiveness of the strategies.

Defining appropriate strategies

When planning a strategy to reinforce appropriate behaviour and to discourage inappropriate behaviour, Table 9.2 can be used.

Table 9.2 *Planning strategies grid*

Planning strategies	
What is the appropriate behaviour for this situation?	
What inappropriate behaviour is affecting this teaching and learning situation?	
Which colleagues can help to analyse the behaviours?	
Which colleagues can help to plan strategies?	
Which strategy/strategies would be most appropriate?	
Who needs to be informed about the strategy/strategies?	
How will the strategy/strategies be introduced?	
How will the strategy/strategies be implemented?	
How will the strategy/strategies be monitored and recorded?	
How will the strategy/strategies be reviewed?	
How will the strategy/strategies be evaluated and modified?	
Who needs to be informed of the process and the progress?	
How will the pupil(s) achievement(s) be recognized, recorded and celebrated?	

Setting targets for reinforcing appropriate behaviour and discouraging inappropriate behaviour

Target-setting is seen as an integral part of the individual education plan (IEP) in the *Code of Practice on the Identification and Assessment of Special Educational Needs* (DfE, 1994b):

Stage 2 – Individual Education Plan

- nature of the child's learning difficulties
- action
  - the special educational provision
  - staff involved, including frequency of support
  - specific programmes/activities/materials/equipment
- help from parents at home
- targets to be achieved in a given time
- any pastoral care or medical requirements
- monitoring and assessment needs
- review arrangements and date.   (para 2:93, p.28)

The process of target-setting can be used as a means of enabling the pupil to discuss what aspects of his or her behaviour need to be addressed and what to aim for. In particular, the following should be considered:

- Does the pupil understand what is appropriate behaviour in that situation?
  - What is expected from the group in that situation?
  - What should he or she be doing?

- Does the pupil understand that his/her behaviour is inappropriate in that situation?
  - Does he or she understand the undesirable effect of his or her behaviour on the rest of the group and on his or her learning?

- What are the targets which can be set for achieving appropriate behaviour?
  - Can the behaviour be broken down into easily achievable parts?

- Does he or she understand them?

- Does the pupil accept them as being realistic?

- What are the rewards for meeting the targets?

A grid for target-setting may be found in Table 3.1 in Chapter 3, Rewards and sanctions.

Here is a simple example:

Brad has been calling out in class without putting his hand up.

- The teacher points out to him that the other children put their hands up when they want to talk to the teacher and wait until they are invited to answer.
- Brad agrees that calling out is unacceptable.
- He agrees that he will try to achieve the targets of:
  - listen to the teacher more carefully
  - put up his hand
  - wait until the teacher asks him for a response
  - says what he wants to say.

- When the targets are met Brad will:
  - receive a merit in his home/school diary
  - show the headteacher or senior member of staff (who *must* show an appropriate response)
  - show his carer.

The teacher, of course must have the target of asking Brad to answer when he raises his hand and to praise him for doing so.

Here is a more complicated example:

Jemima has been wandering around the class, picking up the pens of other children and kicking them when they protest.

- The teacher points out to her that:
  - she is disturbing the others by wandering
  - she is annoying them by interfering with their pens
  - she is hurting them when she kicks them.

- Jemima agrees that:
  - disturbing the others by wandering
  - annoying them by interfering with their pens and
  - hurting them by kicking them
  is unacceptable.

- She agrees that she will try to achieve the targets of:
  - sitting in her seat
  - telling the teacher when she feels restless
  - going straight to the activity when she needs to move round
  - leaving the pens on other children's desks when moving around the class.

- When each target is met Jemima will:
  - receive a merit in her home/school diary
  - show the headteacher or senior member of staff (who *must* show an appropriate response)

  – show her parents.

- When all the targets are met Jemima will receive a certificate, to be presented in the class meeting.

To summarize:

- Describe the behaviours.
- Break the behaviours down into individual behaviours.
- Decide what the child needs to do to overcome each behaviour.
- Set individual targets for each behaviour.
- Agree the rewards.
- Deal with each target one at a time.
- Reward when each one is met.

Counselling

Counselling can be an appropriate strategy for working with the 'difficult pupil' and schools are well-advised to have at least one member of staff who has received training in counselling. The local social services department is often willing to give advice and guidance to schools and educational psychologists, education welfare officers and behaviour consultants can also be involved.

Counselling is used in all kinds of situations in schools today: academic or careers counselling, for example. Often it is used for an informal chat with a pupil. In the sense it is used here, counselling is a highly skilled process which has strict standards of professional competence following advanced training in higher education. However, teachers are often put into the position where they need to use counselling skills and these guidelines should help to ensure that they use their basic skills in relating to pupils effectively:

- If the session is your idea don't jump in with question about 'What's wrong?' (Use comments like, 'You seem very quiet at the moment', 'You seem to be on a short fuse at the moment' to get the conversation going).

- Often pupils will talk more freely if engaged in an activity, like drawing a picture or helping to tidy the classroom.

- Do not touch the pupil or invade the personal space of the pupil.

- Listen.

- Show interest and acceptance (nods and smiles or sympathetic noises).

- Show empathy (understanding with the pupil's position) by using comments like, 'That sounds pretty awful for you', 'That must have made you feel quite hurt', etc.

- Put in connecting comments to encourage further talk – 'What happened next?', 'And then what did you do?'

- Ask how he or she felt about what is being described.

- Do not comment about anything in a negative way.

- Accept what the pupil says as the truth (untruths always come out in the end and there is a reason for them which can tell you a lot about the pupil and how he or she is feeling).

- Do not pry beyond what you are told.

- Do not give advice and do not say what you would do or what someone you know about did.

- Maintain confidentiality as far as you are able; remember though, *if a pupil tells you about possible abuse you must, under The Children Act 1989, pass it on to the Designated Teacher on the staff*. If a pupil asks you to keep it to yourself under these circumstances you must explain that you can't – and why; see Chapter 5, Pupil and staff protection).

- If you feel out of your depth, pass it on to someone else.

- Above all, *make it clear to the pupil that you are on their side* and will try to help if he or she would like you to.

Section 2

Flow chart for the development and implementation of a whole-school behaviour policy

START HERE

The school decides to REVIEW its existing
BEHAVIOUR POLICY or decides
to develop a new one

A **KEY PERSON**
is appointed to oversee the project
(An enthusiastic member of the school's Senior
Management Team)

The **KEY PERSON** meets with the **ACTION GROUP**

NOTE The ACTION GROUP comprises a small group of teachers, support staff and
governors (secondary and upper schools) or all teachers, support staff and some governors
(primary, middle and special schools and Pupil Referral Units [PRUs])

The members of the **ACTION GROUP** read:

Chapters 1–9
Chapter 10, The process of developing and implementing a whole-school behaviour policy
Chapter 11, Establishing shared values

The ACTION GROUP organizes
the review of the school's shared VALUES and
beliefs about how all members of the school
community should behave
Chapter 11, Establishing shared values

The ACTION GROUP REVIEWS
behaviour management in operation throughout the school
Chapter 12 Reviewing the operation of the current behaviour policy

in the classroom   around the school   with individual children

The ACTION GROUP discusses DEVELOPMENT
Chapter 13 Developing a whole-school behaviour policy

Influences from outside the school

IMPLEMENTATION
Chapter 14 Implementing a whole-school behaviour policy

The ACTION GROUP consults with the
whole-school community,
determines PRIORITIES,
maps out the POLICY and draws up
ACTION PLAN and TARGETS

The whole-school community IMPLEMENTS the
WHOLE-SCHOOL BEHAVIOUR POLICY

Chapter 10

The process of developing and implementing a whole-school behaviour policy

In any policy development and implementation, there are four essential elements:

Develop
Implement
Review
Evaluate.

Develop

- The school's behaviour policy should be based on the values and beliefs of teachers, support staff, governors, parents and pupils, on what appropriate behaviour should exist between all members of the school community.

- The policy should have clear *aims* and prioritized objectives expressed as targets within an overall action plan.

- There should be a Key Person (an enthusiastic member of the SMT) responsible for taking the lead in promoting, developing, implementing and reviewing the policy.

- Teachers, support staff, governors, parents and children should be involved in the development and implementation of the policy.

- LEA advisory services, educational psychologists, education welfare officers, academics, researchers and behaviour consultants can help to define priorities and advise on development and implementation.

Implement

- What is the *action plan*?
- What are the long- and short-term targets within the *action plan*?
- Who will be responsible for implementing the *action plan*?
- How will the targets be met?
- Who needs to be consulted/involved/informed?
- What is the timetable?

Review

- Has the *action plan* been implemented?
- Has it fulfilled the *aims* of the policy?
- What criteria will show that the targets have been met?
- Who needs to know that the targets have been met and how can this be reported?
- Does there need to be a new *action plan* and if so, what are the new targets?

Evaluate

- Have the school's shared values about behaviour been demonstrated through the operation of the behaviour policy in practice?
- Is the policy understood and owned by teachers, support staff, governors, parents and children?
- Are the consequent rewards, sanctions and punishments perceived as achievable and fair by the whole school community?

Does the policy work?

The process of developing and implementing a whole-school behaviour policy can be shown diagrammatically, as in Figure 10.1.

Figure 10.1 *Developing and implementing a whole-school behaviour policy*

Stage 1 – Establishing shared values

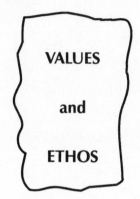

Stage 2 – The review and development cycle, incorporating values and ethos

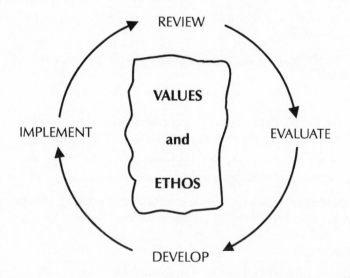

Stage 3 – Influences on the review and development cycle

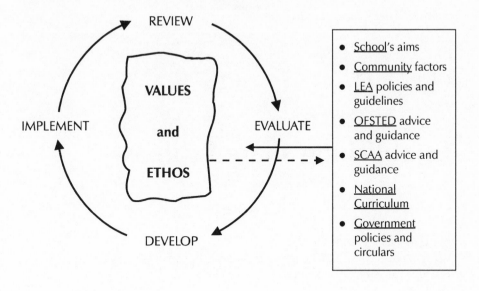

Chapter 11

Establishing shared values

Note to Key Person
Copy pages 104 and 105 back-to-back on thin card (A4) and cut up to make the *nine* cards for this exercise.

A whole-school behaviour policy must be based on the shared values and beliefs that the school community holds about the ways in which members should treat each other. However, it is sometimes difficult to define and prioritize them. To assist this process, the action group can organize the following exercise with the whole staff or do it themselves.

Working in pairs

- look at the six printed cards; place them on a table, along with the three blank cards

- discuss the meanings of the key values shown in lower case lettering on one side of the six cards

- add three key values of your own to the three blank cards

- discuss the statements relating to the key values, shown on the back of the six original cards

- make up three statements relating to your own key values and write them on the back of the cards

- place the resulting nine statements in the shape shown on the next page

LOWEST PRIORITY

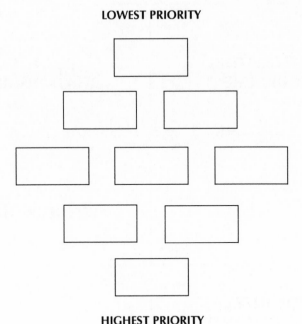

HIGHEST PRIORITY

As a group

Turn the cards over and brainstorm the value statements which have priority for the whole group. List them ready for the next exercise, in Chapter 12.

Behaviour policies are concerned with ensuring that the shared values and beliefs of a school are reflected in the way in which all members of the school community treat each other. The values defined in this exercise should be used as a basis for the review and development of the whole-school behaviour policy.

CELEBRATING ACHIEVEMENT	**POSITIVE RELATIONSHIPS**
	TAKING RESPONSIBILITIES
EQUALITY OF EDUCATIONAL OPPORTUNITY	
	COMMUNITY SPIRIT
EQUAL OPPORTUNITIES	*NOTE ONLY NINE CARDS ARE NEEDED – THROW THIS ONE AWAY*

All members of the school community should behave with respect towards each other	Each pupil's learning achievements should be valued and celebrated by the whole school community
All members of the school community should develop their own self-discipline	
	Every pupil is entitled to a broad and balanced curriculum including the National Curriculum
The school should be known as a caring community within its area	
NOTE *ONLY NINE CARDS ARE* *NEEDED – THROW THIS* *ONE AWAY*	Each member of the school community should be respected as a person, whatever their sex, cultural background, religion, ability or disability

Chapter 12

Reviewing the operation of the current behaviour policy

The review process for the current behaviour policy must involve observations of how it is working throughout the school and the degree to which it is understood and accepted by all members of the school community.

A key question which should be answered by the review process is:

To what extent do:
– teaching and learning;
– relationships between all members of the school community, and
– the behaviour of individual pupils;
reflect the shared values identified in Chapter 11, Establishing shared values?

The Key Person should direct the Action Group in reviewing the operation of the present system:

- in the classroom,
- around the school,
- with individual children.

The grids on pages 109–11 are designed to help in the review process.

In the classroom

Each member of the Action Group should:

- *Read the grid*, 'Checking out the behaviour policy in the classroom' (Figure 12.1, p.109) and think about it for a day or so while going about his or her normal work.

- *Fill it in.* Take about 10 minutes to do this so that initial reactions are recorded.

- *Check.* Does the behaviour observed reflect the shared values and beliefs about the way in which members of the school community should treat each other?
    - with regard to teaching and learning?
    - over routines?
    - as far as pupils relate to each other?
    - as far as adults relate to each other?
    - as far as pupils and adults relate to each other?

- Note any patterns which might be apparent.

- Hand the completed grid to the Key Person.

- A group discussion will be organized by the Key Person.

Concerns which need to be considered in developing the policy will be noted by the Key Person.

Around the school

Each member of the Action Group should:

- *Read the grid,* 'Checking out the behaviour policy around the school' (Figure 12.2, p.110) and think about it for a day or so while going about his or her normal work.

- *Check.* Does the behaviour observed reflect the shared values and beliefs about the way in which members of the school community should treat each other?
    - over routines?
    - as far as pupils relate to each other?
    - as far as adults relate to each other?
    - as far as pupils and adults relate to each other?

- Note any patterns which might be apparent.

- A group discussion will then be organized by the Key Person who will then fill in a consensus grid. This should illustrate the areas of the school outside the classrooms where the behaviour policy needs attention.

Concerns which need to be considered in developing the policy will be noted by the Key Person.

With individual children

Each member of the Action Group should:

- *Fill in* a copy of the 'Checklist of appropriate behaviours' (Figure 12.4, p.112) for each session he or she is involved in, both inside and outside the classroom, for a complete day (lessons, playground duty, dinner time, etc).

- *Fill in* a copy of the 'Checklist of inappropriate behaviours' (Figure 12.5, p.113) for each session he or she is involved in, both inside and outside the classroom, for a complete day.

- *Fill in* the behaviours he or she feels most concerned about on the grid, 'Checking out the behaviour policy with individual pupils' (Figure 12.3, p.111).

- *Check.* Does the behaviour observed reflect the shared values and beliefs about the way in which members of the school community should treat each other?
    - as far as individual pupils relate to other pupils?
    - as far as individual pupils relate to adults?

- Note any patterns which might be apparent.

- A group discussion will be organized by the Key Person. This should illustrate how well the behaviour management policy is working in practice to promote appropriate behaviour.

Concerns which need to be considered in developing the policy will be noted by the Key Person.

Frequency of appropriate and inappropriate behaviour

If necessary, the checklists of appropriate and inappropriate behaviours (Figures 12.4 and 12.5, pp.112–13) can be used to demonstrate the frequency of behaviours. The Action Group could check out the behaviour over a set period of time or, for instance, check every five minutes

At the end of this review exercise, the Key Person and his or her Action Group should be in a position to present a list of concerns to be turned into *priorities for development.*

Figure 12.1

CHECKING OUT THE BEHAVIOUR POLICY IN THE CLASSROOM

Complete this grid. Take about 10 minutes so that you record only your immediate reaction.
Note any pattern which emerges in the rows and columns

KEY: ✓ YES   ✗ NO   N/A Not Applicable   D/K Don't Know

UNDERSTOOD BY:

	RULES	REWARDS	SANCTIONS	PUNISHMENTS	ROUTINES	PERSONAL RESPONSIBILITIES	WHERE TO GO FOR SUPPORT
PUPILS							
PARENTS							
SUPPORT STAFF							
TEACHERS							
HEADS OF DEPT							
HEADTEACHER							

REVIEWED REGULARLY BY:

	RULES	REWARDS	SANCTIONS	PUNISHMENTS	ROUTINES	PERSONAL RESPONSIBILITIES	WHERE TO GO FOR SUPPORT
PUPILS							
PARENTS							
SUPPORT STAFF							
TEACHERS							
HEADS OF DEPT							
HEADTEACHER							

NOTES

Figure 12.2

CHECKING OUT THE BEHAVIOUR POLICY AROUND THE SCHOOL

Complete this grid. Take about 10 minutes so that you record only your immediate reaction.
Note any pattern which emerges in the rows and columns

KEY: ✓ YES   ✗ NO   N/A Not Applicable   D/K Don't Know

UNDERSTOOD BY:

	RULES	REWARDS	SANCTIONS	PUNISHMENTS	ROUTINES	PERSONAL RESPONSIBILITIES	WHERE TO GO FOR SUPPORT
PUPILS							
PARENTS							
SUPPORT STAFF							
TEACHERS							
HEADS OF DEPT							
HEADTEACHER							

REVIEWED REGULARLY BY:

	RULES	REWARDS	SANCTIONS	PUNISHMENTS	ROUTINES	PERSONAL RESPONSIBILITIES	WHERE TO GO FOR SUPPORT
PUPILS							
PARENTS							
SUPPORT STAFF							
TEACHERS							
HEADS OF DEPT							
HEADTEACHER							

NOTES

Figure 12.3

CHECKING OUT THE BEHAVIOUR POLICY WITH INDIVIDUAL PUPILS

TIME: _____ minutes

Mark the relative frequency of the behaviour in the boxes below: 5 = most frequent   1 = least frequent

LOCATION ☞	CLASSROOMS	CORRIDORS	PLAYGROUND	DINING HALL	ASSEMBLIES	OTHER (SPECIFY)	OTHER (SPECIFY)
INAPPROPRIATE BEHAVIOURS ☞							

Figure 12.4

CHECKLIST OF APPROPRIATE BEHAVIOURS

THERE IS ROOM FOR YOUR OWN BEHAVIOURS AT THE BOTTOM

✓ FREQUENCY: **1** = LEAST   **5** = MOST

	1	2	3	4	5
On task					
Moving around in an appropriate manner					
Keeping work place tidy					
Looking after possessions					
Well prepared					
Keeping work safe					
Keen to learn					
Cheerful					
Respecting the cultural differences of others					
Relating appropriately to teachers and other adults					
Listening to teachers/other adults without interruption					
Quiet when asked to be so					
Answering questions appropriately					
Asking relevant questions of teacher/other adult					
Level at which prepared to work at difficult tasks					
Accepting mistakes					
Apologizing for inappropriate behaviour					
Respecting other pupils' space					
Communicating appropriately with other pupils					
Getting on well with other pupils					
Having a community spirit					
Looking after resources and buildings					

Figure 12.5

CHECKLIST OF INAPPROPRIATE BEHAVIOURS

✓ FREQUENCY: **1** = LEAST   **5** = MOST

	1	2	3	4	5
Not staying in seat					
Fidgeting					
Throwing things					
Talking out of turn					
Making unacceptable noises					
Shouting out					
Swearing or using obscene language					
Sulking					
Insolence					
Crying					
Exhibiting racist or sexist behaviour					
Asking inappropriate questions					
Complaining about what he or she is required to do					
Saying he or she cannot do things when he or she can					
Answering the teacher back					
Hiding work or tools					
Destroying own work					
Running out of the session					
Refusing to obey teacher's instructions					
Arguing with the teacher					
Hitting the teacher					
Frightened of teacher or other adult					
Interfering with other pupils					
Hitting other pupils					
Distracting other pupils by talking to them					
Interfering with pupils' work					
Destroying other pupils' work					
Keeping away from other pupils					
Intimidated by other pupils					

SEE BLANK GRID FOR OTHER BEHAVIOURS ON NEXT PAGE

FILL IN OTHER BEHAVIOURS

✓ FREQUENCY: **1** = LEAST   **5** = MOST

	1	2	3	4	5

Chapter 13

Developing a whole-school behaviour policy

The review process will have enabled the Key Person (KP) to list the *concerns* which have come out of the observations of behaviour *in the classroom, around the school* and *with individual pupils*. It might be helpful to keep these three categories to assist with developing the *action plan*.

Everyone in the Action Group (AG) taking part in this review now needs to decide on the *priorities for development* arising from these concerns, under the direction of the Key Person.

The Key Person and the AG need to decide on a time-scale for the development of the policy and to allocate responsibilities for each section within the *framework* outlined below. They also have to decide the frequency and length of the planning sessions.

Deciding on the priorities for development

1. Each member of the AG writes down their own *three concerns* which they feel should become a priority for planning the whole-school behaviour policy.
2. Each member of the AG writes their *first concern* on a flipchart or writing board. A person may write their *second concern* if their first has already been written by someone else. There should be no discussion at this stage.
3. When everyone has listed *one concern*, clarification of meanings can be asked for and discussed within the whole AG.

4. The AG discusses the *concerns* with a view to combine and/or integrate them as much as possible in order to reduce the number.
5. The Key Person rewrites the *concerns* to make them clearer, if necessary.
6. Each member of the group ranks the *concerns*: 1 = most important to 1+ X = least important.
7. The procedure 1–6 is repeated until a consensus emerges which is acceptable to the whole AG and felt to be owned by every member of it.

These *concerns* can now be used to form the basis for the *priorities for development* within a *framework* for the whole-school behaviour policy.

A suggested framework for the whole-school behaviour policy

Date

The date it was compiled, the date(s) it has been reviewed, the frequency of review and the date of the next review.

The development group

A note of the Action Group responsible for its formation: teachers, support staff and governors, together with the name of the Key Person, responsible for collating and writing the policy and for the policy's review and evaluation process.

A statement of shared values and beliefs

What the school community believes about the way pupils and teachers should behave towards one another and the way in which appropriate and inappropriate behaviour should be handled.

The aims

The aims of the policy: what the policy is designed to achieve.

The areas to be covered by the behaviour policy

A list of the areas to be covered, together with the basic principles within which the policy will work. These could be the areas outlined in the first part of this book:

- Teaching and learning (Chapter 2)
- Rewards and sanctions (Chapter 3)
- Bullying (Chapter 4)
- Pupil and staff protection (Chapter 5)
- Equal opportunities (Chapter 6)
- Involving parents (Chapter 7)
- Support for all (Chapter 8).

There then needs to be a set of procedures through which the policy operates within these different areas. These could include:

- Procedures for teaching and learning (Chapter 2)
    - the accepted routines for teaching and learning,
    - the need for consistency of response to achievement and learning difficulties from the adults in the school,
    - how pupils and staff communicate with each other.

- Procedures for rewards and sanctions (Chapter 3)
    - target-setting for each pupil in learning and behaviour,
    - the use of praise and encouragement,
    - the use of rewards for achievement (related to each child's individual targets),
    - the celebration of achievement in learning and behaviour,
    - the way in which pupils are brought face-to-face with the consequences of their inappropriate behaviour,
    - the way reparation works,
    - the system of sanctions (related to each pupil's individual targets),
    - the system of punishments in operation,
    - care of buildings, grounds and resources.

  Note: these points should be related to other school policies, in particular those on the curriculum, parental involvement and health and safety.

- Procedures on bullying (Chapter 4)
  The procedures could include reference to guidelines and procedures for bullying, related to the prevention of bullying and the link with personal and social development.

- Pupil and staff protection (Chapter 5)
  The procedures could contain guidance to pupils on *keeping safe* and should give information on who they can talk to and contact if they are worried about any incident, at home or at school, whether involving another pupil or an adult.

  All schools should, in accordance with The Children Act 1989 (HMSO, 1989), have a Designated Teacher who is responsible for overseeing the child protection requirements of the Act within the school.

All staff should be aware of the identity of the Designated Teacher and his or her role in the school. Policies should emphasize that any suspicions regarding possible abuse or assault should be referred immediately to the Designated Teacher, who will take the appropriate action.

The government's Circular 10/95 (DfEE, 1995a) and the LEA's guidelines on child protection should be used to check the school's proposed framework and the specific local organization. Reference should also be made to the sections on child protection in the OFSTED Handbooks on the inspection of nursery and primary schools (1995a, p.93); secondary schools (1995b, p.98) and special schools (1995c, p.99).

- Procedures for physical control and restraint (Chapter 5)
  There must be clear procedures for physical control and restraint and these must be in accordance with official government and LEA policies. These procedures should be regularly reviewed and approved by the governors as official school policy.

- Procedures for protecting staff from false allegations (Chapter 5)
  The procedures should give staff clear guidelines on protecting themselves from allegations of abuse or assault against pupils.

- Procedures for written records (Chapter 5)
  There should be guidelines and procedures for written records of any inappropriate behaviour which involves physical contact and/or injury to pupils or to staff, or any serious damage to property. All such incidents must be recorded in the school's 'Incident book' or 'Day book' or wherever the school records such incidents. (See the report forms in Figures 5.2 and 5.3.)

Note: schools have to keep records in permanent book form. Any recording sheets used for incidents should be copied into such a book. In the case of injury to pupils or to staff, statements should be taken from each pupil and member of staff present.

At all times, the action laid down in the school's and LEA's disciplinary procedures should be followed, and statutory requirements met.

Note: it might well be appropriate for schools to have separate policies for bullying and child protection but they need to be referenced within the whole-school behaviour policy. A sample whole-school behaviour policy can be found in Appendix I.

Other useful materials

These may be found in *Discipline in Schools, The Elton Report* (DES, 1989a):

Appendix F1   Code of Conduct (extract from a booklet for pupils) p.283
Appendix F2   Classroom Expectations (guidance for pupils displayed in a classroom) p.284
Appendix F3   Rewards and Sanctions (extracts from a booklet for teachers) p.286
Appendix F4   Inside Information – The Way to Good Order (a booklet for staff) p.289.

Chapter 14

Implementing a whole-school behaviour policy

Any form of whole-school policy implies consensus, but even when consensus appears to have been reached there can be differing understanding and interpretations as to the precise implications of what has been 'agreed'. A structured approach to implementation, with a formal action plan and set targets, can help to keep the implementation on schedule and maintain common ownership.

The *action plan* for implementing the whole-school behaviour policy can be organized under the following headings:

What?
How?
Who?
When?

Within each of these areas it will be helpful to consider possible problems and possible solutions.

What?
- What are the *targets* to be achieved?
- What action needs to be taken to achieve these *targets*?
- What steps can this action be divided into?
- What is needed in terms of staffing, resources, accommodation?
- What are the evaluation criteria?

How?
- How will the *targets* be achieved within the *action plan*?
- How will the effectiveness of the *action plan* be assessed?

- How can all members of the school community become involved in the *action plan*?
- How will the effectiveness of the policy be reviewed?

Who?
- Who should be informed about the *action plan* and *targets*?
- Who has responsibility for each *target* in the *action plan*?
- Who else needs to be involved? Teachers? Support staff? Governors? Parents? Pupils? Other agencies? The LEA?
- Who will identify the resources needed and allocate them appropriately?
- Who will be responsible for evaluating the effectiveness of the policy?

When?
- When will the completion date of the *action plan* be?
- When will each *target* be met?
- When will the resources be needed?
- When will the new policy be in operation?
- When will the new policy be reviewed?
- When will the new policy be evaluated?

For all the above points you need to consider:

Possible problems –
- Definition of tasks.
- Delegation of tasks.
- Methodology.
- Resourcing/accommodation.
- Timing.

Possible solutions –
- Make the development and implementation of a whole-school behaviour policy a priority in the school development plan.

- Consult the whole school community well in advance about the policy and the timetable for its implementation.

- Set clear, realistic *targets*.

- Share responsibility under the direction of the Key Person (an enthusiastic member of the school's SMT).

- Use the exercise 'Deciding on priorities for development' in Chapter 13, Developing a whole-school behaviour policy, as a basis for deciding on targets.

- Use a time-line to help with timing and sequencing.

- Set effectiveness indicators as part of the *action plan* in order to assist evaluation.

The precise structure for planning all this will depend on the way in which a particular school operates its review and development. A suggested plan for the implementation of the whole-school behaviour policy may be found in Figure 14.1.

Planning level	Participants	Purposes	Outcomes
Long-term Total period of time agreed for implementation One year?	Headteacher, Key Person and Action Group	A broad framework for the implementation of policy regarding: • behaviour policy within the classroom • behaviour policy around the school • behaviour policy with individual pupils incorporating or ensuring compatibility with: • bullying policy • child protection policy	Staff ownership of practices specified within the policy A fully functioning whole-school behaviour policy
Medium-term Termly or half-termly plans?	Headteacher, Key Person, Action Group, subject coordinators/ heads of department, all staff and governors	To develop specific targets within an overall action plan To examine possible snags and strategies for overcoming them	Planning of behaviour policy objectives into curriculum plans Staff trained in positive approaches to behaviour management
Short-term Weekly or daily plans?	All teachers and support assistants	To relate behaviour policy to: • classroom management practice • teaching and learning within subject areas • staff/pupil relationships	Staff skilled in positive approaches to behaviour

Figure 14.1 *Plan for implementing a whole-school behaviour policy*

Note to Key Person: use the grid in Figure 14.2 to help brainstorm and develop the action plan within the Action Group.

	What?	How?	Who?	When?	Possible problems	Possible solutions
Targets • • • • • • •					*What?* *How?* *Who?* *When?*	*What?* *How?* *Who?* *When?*
Action • • • • • • •					*What?* *How?* *Who?* *When?*	*What?* *How?* *Who?* *When?*
Resources • • • • • • •					*What?* *How?* *Who?* *When?*	*What?* *How?* *Who?* *When?*

Figure 14.2 *Action plan for a whole-school behaviour policy*

Appendix I
A sample policy for behaviour

Date of policy: _____

Date of reviews: _____

Key Person: _____

Action Group: _____

_____

_____

The school's shared values and beliefs about behaviour

The members of this school community believe that:

> *The way children and adults behave depends on the way they feel about themselves*
>
> *The way children and adults feel about themselves depends on the way in which those around them respond to their behaviour*

- Pupils who feel that they are unvalued, worthless and that they are failures tend to express these feelings in the form of inappropriate behaviour.

- Pupils who feel valued, cared about and successful tend to behave appropriately.

- Pupils learn very quickly that if they behave in a certain way, they will be treated in a certain way.

- When pupils are treated inconsistently, they are unable to distinguish between desirable and undesirable behaviour.

- Pupils also learn that they can often get their own way if they behave inappropriately.

- If the ethos of the classroom and the school is positive then there will already be an atmosphere of mutual respect and self-esteem enhancement in which pupils are behaving appropriately and teaching and learning is leading to achievement.

The aims of the behaviour policy

- To make all members of the school community feel valued, secure and to be successful in teaching and learning.

- To encourage appropriate behaviour between all members of the school community.

Areas covered by this behaviour policy

The school's behaviour policy centres on the following main sections.

Shared routines in teaching and learning

- Staff will establish shared routines for teaching and learning within which all members of the school community feel secure and to enable behaviour to be consistent and fair.

For pupils who behave inappropriately, routines offer a framework of security in which they can succeed in relating to adults and to learning.

Routines are crucial to the establishment of effective teaching and learning. Individual departments and teaching groups will establish their own routines for effective teaching and learning.

(See 'Procedures for establishing and maintaining routines for teaching and learning' at the end of this policy.)

The celebration and reward of achievement

- All pupils will receive appropriate commendation and rewards for achieving against their own personal targets in learning and in behaviour.

Pupils who feel that their work or their appropriate behaviour is not valued will lose motivation and will give up trying.

All pupils will have the chance to succeed in learning and in behaviour.

(See 'Procedures for celebrating and rewarding achievement' at the end of this policy.)

Rewards, sanctions and punishments

- A system of rewards, sanctions and punishments which is accepted as fair and reasonable for the whole school community and which is routinely practised.

Rewards make acceptable behaviour more likely to be repeated. Punishments make undesirable behaviour less likely to be repeated. Sanctions give the opportunity to negotiate reparation and to set targets for desirable behaviour.

(See 'Procedures for rewards, sanctions and punishments' at the end of this policy.)

Bullying

- All bullying will be identified within the school community and it will be dealt with effectively.

Bullying is not acceptable behaviour in this school. All pupils and adults have rights and responsibilities in the way in which they behave towards each other and the way in which they make each other feel.

Bullying will be monitored and will be dealt with as soon as it occurs.

(See 'Procedures for dealing with bullying' at the end of this policy.)

Keeping safe

- All members of the school community will be kept safe through effective procedures for child and adult protection.

All pupils and adults need to feel safe when they relate to each other within the school.

The school will follow all statutory, government guidelines and LEA guidelines on child protection.

(See 'Procedures for keeping safe' at the end of this policy.)

Equality of educational opportunity

- Equality of educational opportunity will be ensured as far as is practicable for all pupils who are behaving inappropriately.

Children who behave inappropriately are often excluded from lessons or even from the school community. This has serious implications as far as equality of educational opportunity is concerned.

Often, boys are excluded from learning more than girls and this must be taken into account.

Behavioural norms vary between different ethnic groups and this must be borne in mind when deciding on whether or not behaviour is appropriate within a given situation.

(See 'Procedures for equal opportunities' at the end of this policy.)

Parental involvement

- Parents will be positively involved in all aspects of their children's inappropriate behaviour in school.

The school will establish who has parental responsibility and who each pupil's parent or carer is.

Parents will be as fully involved in behaviour and learning as possible.

(See 'Procedures for involving parents' at the end of the policy.)

Procedures for establishing shared routines for teaching and learning

The following do's and don'ts will be adopted by all teachers in the classroom:

Do:

- Have the work well prepared, including specially differentiated materials for pupils who are likely to find it difficult.

- Make sure the room is laid out as you want it and that all the materials and equipment are ready for use.

- Establish and insist on routines for:
    - entering the classroom,
    - putting bags and coats away,
    - seating arrangements,
    - explaining the tasks ahead,
    - equipment needed,
    - giving out work/books,
    - setting out work,
    - listening to the teacher,
    - listening to other pupils,
    - questions and answers,
    - cooperative work,

  - stopping work,
  - summarizing the session,
  - giving out homework,
  - leaving the classroom to go to the toilet,
  - clearing up,
  - packing up and leaving the classroom.

- Know and use the pupils' names.

- Treat the pupils as responsible and valued human beings.

- Establish positive norms of behaviour – 'This is how we behave in here'.

- Concentrate on the work in hand.

- Ignore inappropriate behaviour as far as possible.

- Praise and encourage those who are working well.

- Use eye contact or a hand gesture to express disapproval.

- Have a quiet word with the pupil that the behaviour is inappropriate and should stop.

- Try to maintain a good level of humour – learning is fun!

- Describe the effects of the behaviour not the behaviour itself ('When you call out it disturbs the others', 'When you make a noise the class can't hear', etc).

- Send for help in good time.

- Ask for a pupil to be withdrawn.

- Allow time for a pupil to unwind before he or she is asked to make amends.

- Follow up any inappropriate behaviour with the pupil on their own.

Don't:
- Start the lesson until all the pupils are ready.

- Talk above the background noise.

- Shout.

- Make sarcastic or hurtful comments about pupils.

- Deal with disruptive behaviour or set targets for behaviour in front of other pupils.

- Allow pupils to sit where they want to sit.

- Allow pupils to wear coats or keep bags on the work tables.
- Finish the lesson in a rush without summarizing what has been covered.
- Draw unnecessary attention to inappropriate behaviour.
- Provoke confrontations.
- Make any physical contact with the pupils.
- Interview a pupil in a closed room alone.

Procedures for the celebration and reward of achievement

Staff will reward and celebrate achievement by:

- Making the pupil aware of success throughout each lesson.
- Talking about successes at the end of the lesson.
- Positive comments in the pupil's 'Achievement book'.
- Asking the pupil to show their work/Achievement book to a visitor or a senior member of staff.
- Pointing out achievement to the rest of the group.
- Taking work or the Achievement book or a note home to parents/carers.
- A 'mention' in assembly or tutor group meeting.
- Charts on the wall.
- Work displayed.
- Photographs and/or videos.
- Using a pupil's personal Record of Achievement book.
- *Good News!* cards home to parents/carers (see p.77).

Teachers will have positive feedback on their performance from the heads of departments and the senior management team (SMT).

Procedures for rewards, sanctions and punishments

It should be noted that rewards are more likely to be effective if:

- They are given immediately.
- It is clear what the reward is for.

- They are related to inappropriate behaviour which worries the pupil.
- They relate to small target steps in achievement.
- The targets are agreed between teacher and pupil and reviewed regularly.

Targets

Adults will define inappropriate behaviour in terms of what the pupil has been observed doing; once behaviour has been described in these terms, it is easier to set targets. Remember:

- the process of setting targets will be agreed between all members of staff
- each pupil will have individual targets
- targets will be set for achieving appropriate behaviour – not for stopping the inappropriate behaviour
- targets will be realistic and not intimidatory: the pupil will reject any target he or she sees as unobtainable
- a senior member of staff will monitor target-setting in order to achieve consistency.

Rewards

Teachers can reward personally and immediately by:

- encouraging
- smiling and nodding
- a positive tone of voice
- praise
- being near to the pupil
- positive comments on work.

Teachers can reward by giving 'treats':

- special privileges
- trophies
- extra play/break time
- choosing favourite activities.

Alternatively, the teacher could award something which conveys approval and status:

- badges
- merit awards
- certificates
- team/house points
- photographs
- sending *Good News!* cards home to parents/carers (see p.77).

A framework for rewards

Pupils will be rewarded for meeting targets in:

- *changing inappropriate behaviour into appropriate behaviour*
- *achievement in learning: academic, personal and social.*

Rewards will be organized in a series of levels:

Level 1: Praise and encouragement
- to the pupil
- involving any adults visiting the group
- in assembly/class meeting.

Level 2: Merits
- certificates
- tokens
- comments in a book
- on a chart on the wall.

The merits will be:
- mentioned in assembly or tutor group meeting
- stamped with a symbol or have a sticky stamp affixed by a senior member of staff
- recorded on a chart on the wall of the tutor group room
- taken home to show parents/carers
- mentioned in a Good News! card home to parents/carers.

Level 3: Certificates of achievement
These will be awarded for ten merits and:
- will be presented in assembly
- will be copied for display in the tutor/classroom
- will be copied to take home
- the pupil will be photographed with the certificate and the photograph displayed in the entrance area of the school and a copy taken home.

Remember: if the pupils' targets are set at the right level for each pupil then every pupil should regularly meet the targets set and hence achieve rewards.

Sanctions

All pupils must be confronted with the unacceptable nature of their behaviour and sanctions should be imposed in order to get them to recognize the behaviour as unreasonable and unacceptable and to make some attempt to make amends:

'OK, this is what you have done…'
'How should you have behaved?'
'How are you going to behave in future?' and, as appropriate,
'How are you going to put things right?'

Possibilities for 'putting things right' should be negotiated according to the pupil's behaviour targets.

Putting things right might include:

- apologizing,
- making up lost work in free time,
- repairing damage caused.

Whatever other considerations apply, sanctions imposed too long after an 'offence' or for too long, simply reinforce resentment and the pupil's feelings of badness and rejection. After a while, ongoing sanctions do not mean anything.

Sanctions should be:

- immediate
- related to the behavioural targets of that pupil (where appropriate)
- focused on the behaviour, not on the child as a person
- perceived as fair
- such that they give an opportunity for putting things right (reparation).

Afterwards:

- the slate should be wiped clean
- a fresh start should be made by all concerned.

Withdrawal

Withdrawal could be seen as punishing the pupil by exclusion. It should only be used for those pupils whose behaviour affects the learning of others to a serious extent.

For withdrawal to be effective:

- the teaching or activity group must be seen as a more desirable place to be than the place to which the pupil is withdrawn
- it must be as 'antiseptic' as possible
- there should not be an audience
- it should be for the shortest possible time
- it should be complete in itself.

Note: some pupils may work for withdrawal in order to avoid work or what are perceived as unpleasant experiences. There is no real answer to this, apart from making the withdrawal as routine, non-confrontational and 'antiseptic' as possible: *not in haste – not in anger.*

Procedure for withdrawal

1. The undesirability of the behaviour will be discussed with the pupil and he or she will be requested to stop
    - 'This is what you are doing'
    - 'It is disturbing others'
    - 'Please stop'.

2. If the undesirable behaviour continues, the pupil will be warned that, if he or she does not stop, they will have to be withdrawn
    - 'You are still disturbing the group. If you continue, you will have to go out'.

3. If the undesirable behaviour still continues, assistance should be sought from the teacher on call. That person will remove the pupil from the room.

4. If the pupil is in a calm state and simply needs a period of 'time-out', he or she will sit in a suitable room – one with no audience, which is quiet and which offers as little stimulation as possible.

    If he or she is in an angry or distressed state, he or she needs to be supervised by an adult.

    If any form of physical restraint is necessary, the school and local authority's official policies and guidelines on physical control and re-straint will be followed rigorously and an 'Incident report form' should be used and a record made in the school's 'Incident book'. The incident should be discussed with the child's parents/carers as soon as possible.

5. Sooner or later the pupil will be able to talk about his or her behaviour in the classroom with the supervising adult. The following should be discussed:
    - what the inappropriate behaviour was
    - what the appropriate behaviour would have been
    - how things can be put right
    - how he or she will behave when he or she returns to the group.

6. When the pupil returns to the group, the teacher should welcome him or her back and the incident is then *closed*.

7. If the same pupil is obviously unable to settle in class without seriously affecting the learning of the other pupils that day, he or she will be taken

home for the rest of the day (or remain at home the next day, if it is late on in the day)
- 'I am sorry but you are just not coping and you will have to go home'. The difficulties should be discussed with the pupil on his or her return to school as in Point 5 (above).
8. The incident should be logged in the school's 'Incident book'.

A flowchart (shown in Figure 3.1, p.41) will be placed on the wall of each teaching area.

Punishments

If the behaviour is such that the staff feel that the pupil needs to be punished then the following punishments will be used, following these guidelines at all times:

Lines
Lines should not be frivolous or offensive. They should relate in some way to the inappropriate behaviour and be as 'antiseptic' as possible.

Work around the school
It is questionable if a pupil will keep the school any tidier if made to pick up litter, but it does help to keep the school looking good.

Extra school work
Disaffected pupils are not likely to become more motivated about school work if they are given more of it. On the other hand, if the pupil achieves at the work task then they can be positive.

On report
Unfortunately reports are usually used as a record of misdemeanours and to make a spectacle of the pupil concerned. The report system will be used in a positive way to help set targets and to enable children to make amends.

Detentions
The main problem with detentions is that there tend to be a few regular teachers who make use of them and it is colleagues, especially SMT colleagues, who end up taking them. This problem will be alleviated by making sure that it is only the staff who use the system who run detentions.

Involvement of parents/carers

Parents/carers are often only involved at crisis point. They will be involved earlier rather than later on in proceedings.

Children hate and react against 'complaints' to parents/carers and parents/carers do not like to be made to feel responsible for inappropriate behaviour in school.

Remember that some pupils who exhibit more disturbing behaviour have a poor relationship with their parents/carers who can use a negative letter home as an excuse to further reject their children or even to physically chastise them.

Parents/carers will be informed about punishments for more serious offences and given reasonable notice of detentions.

All letters to parents/carers will be positive in tone and not seek to blame them for the inappropriate behaviour.

Informing parents/carers about inappropriate behaviour has a deterrent effect. They will be asked for their comments, suggestions and advice.

It should be borne in mind that parents who have to stay at home to look after excluded or withdrawn pupils can lose money from work.

Withdrawal of privileges

Pushed to its logical conclusion, the pupil who behaves inappropriately for most of the time will have no privileges and will not, for example, go on any trips. Care will be taken that the withdrawal of a privilege is the punishment for one incident. Withdrawal of privileges will not be made as a result of adding up incidents.

In practice, if inappropriate behaviour is dealt with positively through the setting of appropriate targets, and a fresh start made, then children should take part in all privileged activities – but will be withdrawn from them if they demonstrate that they cannot cope with them.

Exclusions

Exclusions do not endear the school to disaffected pupils. The longer they are excluded, the longer it will take to reassimilate them.

They often go on for far too long. It is the initial stage of exclusion which punishes; any prolonging leads to further disaffection.

Care will be taken that the pupil feels that the punishment is complete in itself and that they can make a fresh stage with no recriminations when they return.

Whatever form of punishment is used:

- it should be in proportion to the incident
- it should be clearly understood and accepted by the pupil and his or her parents/carers – and seen as fair and reasonable

- it should be as 'antiseptic' as possible

- it should be complete in itself

- it should not increase the status of the pupil within the peer group or the family (for example, make him or her a martyr)

- it will be monitored by a member of the SMT in order to make sure that all members of staff are acting within the guidelines of the whole-school behaviour policy and are fair and consistent

- it will be recorded in the teacher's own record book, which will be monitored by a member of the SMT and governors

- serious incidents and punishments will be recorded on an 'Incident report form' and in the school's 'Incident book'.

In general, punishments will not be given in anger or in haste and will be as 'antiseptic' as possible: 'You have done this –', 'This is the punishment'.

Procedures for dealing with bullying

Evidence of bullying will be gathered from a wide variety of sources on an ongoing basis, including:

- Observations of behaviour throughout the school.

- Discussions with pupils and staff.

- Records from the school's 'Incident report form' and in the school's 'Incident book'.

- 'Worries' from pupils.

- Complaints from parents, carers or social workers.

- The pupil survey at the end of this section. (This will be given to a sample of pupils from at least one group from each year every other term.)

Responses to bullying

- the school will establish a clear policy on equality of opportunity based on the shared belief within the school community that all members of the community are of equal worth and have rights and responsibilities towards each other

- the affective curriculum will include, within its personal and social development programme, training on 'Keeping safe', and on the equal worth of all individuals within the school community, irrespective of race, gender, disability, ability, learning difficulties, behaviour difficulties, appearance or cultural background. Pupils will also be taught how to be assertive

– within courses designed to promote spiritual and moral development, pupils will be taught about rights and responsibilities within communities

– the school will regularly monitor the amount of bullying going on

– pupils will be encouraged to make their concerns known to a member of staff. This will form part of the 'Worry sheet' procedure (see below)

– pupils should feel confident that their concerns will be taken seriously and that they will not be made worse by the action taken

– staff should be careful that they treat each other with respect in front of the children

– staff should treat pupils with respect and not bully them in the teaching and learning situation or around the school

– staff should be careful to show disapproval of the bully without bullying the bully. They should separate the pupil from the behaviour and make it clear that it is the behaviour which is not wanted, and that they do want the pupil

– bullies must be brought face-to-face with the consequences of their bullying on the victim (but not by being bullied by adults)

– bullies will be involved in working out how to make amends

– attention will be paid to helping to raise the self-esteem of victims and bullies

– parents/carers will be involved in seeking solutions to their children's victimization or bullying

– a record of all bullying will be maintained in the school's 'Incident book'

– the school's education welfare officer, educational psychologists and an independent behaviour consultant will be used to provide advice and guidance to staff and pupils, as appropriate.

Bullied adults

The SMT will work towards enabling each adult in the school to:

– reflect positively on their own performance

- recognize their strengths
- use these strengths in overcoming weaknesses in other areas
- feel useful within the school community
- feel valued within the school community.

Procedures for keeping safe

Adults within the school will receive training in how to:

- remain pupil-focused at all times;
- recognize the signs of abuse and what to do about them;
- be able to develop working practices which minimize the risk of being accused of abusing pupils;
- take the necessary steps to protect themselves from false allegations;
- deal with any false allegations which might be made against them.

Any adult who suspects abuse will:

- *listen* to what the pupil says; and
- make detailed factual notes on an 'Incident report form' (p.00) to pass on to the school's Designated Teacher (see below). A sketch showing the site and extent of any visible injuries is often useful;
- *remember* that any notes might subsequently be used in criminal proceedings;
- *inform the school's Designated Teacher immediately.*

On no account should the suspecting adult attempt to interview the pupil, examine the pupil physically, gather any other evidence or contact parents/carers. This could have serious implications for any possible future criminal proceedings.

Do not attempt to deal with it alone – pass it on to the Designated Teacher.

The school's Designated Teacher is: _____

The Designated Teacher

As required by The Children Act 1989, the school has a Designated Teacher, who is responsible for monitoring child protection issues in the school, maintaining links with the *area child protection committee* (ACPC), the social services department and the Local Education Authority.

The duties of the Designated Teacher are to:

- keep records of child protection issues and concerns and to be aware of the legal status of such records;

- be aware of the signs and symptoms of abuse and when to make a referral (*when in doubt* to seek the advice of the social services department, the NSPCC or, where appropriate, the local education authority's *Child Protection Coordinator*);

- regularly monitor and review all pupils who are on the *Child Protection Register* and/or are the subjects of emergency protection orders, care orders or supervision orders;

- inform all relevant staff of all pupils on the *Child Protection Register*, including the school's education welfare officer;

- pass information to the new school when a pupil leaves, and inform the custodian of the *Child Protection Register* of the change (the social services department or NSPCC on behalf of the social services department);

- ensure that **all** staff receive training on child protection and on the requirements of The Children Act 1989, including how to report suspicions;

- keep **all** staff informed about child protection issues;

- develop effective links with other agencies and support services.

In a case of suspected child abuse the Designated Teacher should:

- make sure that all relevant evidence is recorded on the same day – observations, quotes, records of any conversations with the pupil and any other concerned persons. *Note*: on no account should any pupil or adult be asked to write a statement themselves, although it is permissible for the Designated Teacher to make notes of any statements, conversations or relevant 'Incident report forms'; and to record these in the school's 'Incident book';

- inform the social services department or NSPCC of the circumstances – if necessary the emergency duty team. (Note: the social services department or the NSPCC will inform the police);

- send a written report to the social worker who deals with the case as soon as possible. Remember that the pupil's parent(s)/carer(s) may have access to this report in any subsequent child protection conference and/or court proceedings.
  Note: All reports should be based on *evidence*, distinguishing between fact, observations made, reports of conversations, allegations and opinion. Reports will include details of:
  - educational progress and achievements
  - attendance
  - behaviour

- participation in school activities
- relations with other pupils and adults
- where relevant: family structure and what is known of the pupil's position in the family.

- attend any subsequent *Child Protection Conference* or arrange for a representative to attend. Prior to the conference, a report should be sent for consideration. The representative will be someone like the class teacher or group tutor, who knows the child well;

- if a pupil's name is placed on the *Child Protection Register*, ensure that an appropriate member of staff becomes a member of the Core Group and is available to attend all Core Group meetings.

A *Core Group* is appointed at the *Child Protection Conference* and is responsible for ensuring the implementation of the child's own *Child Protection Plan*, which is formulated to ensure that any risk of 'significant harm' to the child is eliminated.

Keeping safe

Just as in situations of bullying (see above), pupils need to know who they can turn to in confidence if they are concerned about the way in which they are being treated. This will form an integral part of the school's personal and social education curriculum.

A 'Worry sheet' (see Figure 5.1, p.58) will be pinned in each teaching space and in the back of each pupil's daily log, giving the names and telephone numbers of those who can help.

Physical restraint and control

The Children Act 1989 states that in any legal proceedings, 'the child's welfare shall be the court's paramount consideration'.

Care sometimes implies physical control and staff should at all times be aware of the levels of permissible control and their responsibilities to the pupils they are working with. At the same time, they need to protect themselves.

The Local Education Authority has a policy on the permissible forms of physical control and restraint and this is appended to this whole school behaviour policy and recognized as official school policy by the governors.

The following guidelines should be followed at all times:

Adults working with children are only authorised to employ physical restraint where:

- they believe that all other alternatives have failed;

- pupils are at risk of physical injury;
- a pupil's actions are placing other pupils or adults at the risk of injury;
- significant damage to property can be limited.

Physical restraint must not endanger the physical safety of pupils or staff.

In addition:

- the level of force must be the *minimum* necessary to ensure the safety of the children and adults;
- it is illegal to hit pupils in any circumstances;
- only approved methods of handling must be used and the headteacher will ensure that staff receive regular training;
- a second adult should be involved wherever possible in order to protect the pupils and adults;
- the incident should be reported to the Designated Teacher;
- any incidents of inappropriate behaviour involving the welfare of pupils and adults, any incidents of violence between pupils and staff, including any incidents of physical restraint and serious damage to property, *must* be recorded on 'Physical restraint report forms' (see p.00) and in the school's 'Incident book';
- in the case of injury to any pupil or adult, notes should be taken of interviews with each pupil and adult present. On no account should any pupil or adult be asked to write a statement. The Designated Teacher will liaise with parents/carers, police and the social services department, where appropriate.

The school will protect the staff by:

- making sure that staff receive training on child protection issues, including protecting themselves from false allegations;
- having clear guidelines on the physical care and control of pupils which have been passed as official school policy by the governors;
- having clear guidelines on procedures for dealing with incidents of child abuse;
- encouraging staff to seek the legal protection of a trade union or third party insurance;
- supporting accused staff by offering counselling and advice;
- arranging independent counselling for school staffs which have an accused colleague, possibly from an independent child protection consultant;
- appointing a governor with responsibility for child protection;
- making sure that all incidents are logged on 'Incident report forms', 'Physical restraint report forms' (see pp.64–5) and in the school's 'Incident book'

The adults working in this school should be aware that they can protect themselves by:

- not putting themselves into potentially compromising situations (eg, alone in a changing room with a pupil with the door closed);
- never physically controlling or restraining a pupil alone;
- reporting any injuries sustained in school to the Designated Teacher and making a record on 'Incident report forms' and 'Physical restraint report forms' (see pp.64–5) and in the school's 'Incident book';
- joining a trade union which has a clear policy on staff protection and which employs specialist legal help if necessary;
- always taking a 'friend' (for example, a union official to any meeting where conduct over the handling of a pupil is questioned);
- making detailed, personal notes of any incident, together with any statements from witnesses at the time, and keeping a diary of all information which subsequently comes to light.

When a member of staff is accused of abusing a child:

- the guidelines given on suspension of staff in the government Circular 10/95, Annex: *Teachers and Child Protection; Teachers facing an allegation of physical/sexual abuse; Guidelines on practice and procedure* (p.15) will be adhered to at all times;
- it is the responsibility of the headteacher (the governors, in the case of allegations against the headteacher) to decide whether or not to suspend the accused person and the prime considerations will be the continuing safety of the pupils, the possibilities of tampering with evidence, the interests of the person concerned and of the school. Although such suspensions are 'without prejudice', any suspension is seen by the pupils, parents/carers and the general public at large as implying guilt. Consequently, suspensions will be avoided wherever possible;
- the full evidence, including witness statements, will be made available to the person in question without delay;
- where an allegation is made by a pupil or parent, the pupil in question will not be allowed contact with the accused person or with any potential witnesses;
- members of staff who make allegations about another member of staff concerning the possible abuse of a pupil will not be allowed to continue working with that pupil, his or her parents/carers or with potential witnesses, while investigations are proceeding;
- members of staff who make allegations about another member of staff concerning the possible abuse of a pupil will not be seen to benefit from them and will be disciplined if the allegations are found to be malicious;

- adults who are accused of abusing a pupil and the school staff will have access to supportive counselling services, possibly from an independent child protection consultant;
- the member of the school's governing body with responsibility for child protection will keep in touch with accused members of staff.

Written records

The following should be recorded on 'Incident report forms' or 'Physical restraint report forms' (see Figures 5.2 and 5.3, pp.64–5) and *must* then be written in the school's 'Incident book':

- any inappropriate behaviour which involves physical contact and/or injury between pupils or staff;
- any serious damage to property;
- any physical restraint used.

The accounts *must* include:

- the time and place of the incident;
- the antecedents of the incident;
- exactly what happened;
- the consequences of the incident, including a note of all injuries sustained by staff and/or pupils and any serious damage to property;
- in the case of serious injury and/or damage to property, names of all witnesses and notes of any interviews with witnesses. Written statements must not be taken from pupils or adults.

Note: The 'Incident book', together with any 'Incident report forms' or 'Physical restraint report forms' *must* be kept available for inspection by the governors, any officials of the Local Education Authority and OFSTED inspectors who have a right to see it.

Procedures for equal opportunities

When a pupil is excluded from a lesson:

- The staff concerned should inform the pupil's group tutor.
- The procedures laid down for withdrawal in 'Procedures for rewards, sanctions and punishments' should be followed as far as resolving the issues surrounding the exclusion.
- Any work which is missed must be covered as fully as possible with the pupil.

When a pupil is excluded from school, the school maintains a responsibility to reintegrate the pupil as soon as possible (see the guidelines in 'Procedures for rewards, sanctions and punishments'). The school has a responsibility in the meantime for maintaining access to the curriculum.

The group tutor is responsible for ensuring that appropriate work is made available to the pupil from the teachers who normally teach him or her and for ensuring that any support teacher is given it. He or she is also responsible for monitoring the progress of the pupil and for ensuring that the work is marked.

Procedures for involving parents

Parents or carers?

Remember that the pupil might live with a carer or a step-parent. Use the child's own names for the adults at home when talking to them – 'What did Mum say?', 'What did Fred [Mum's partner] say?'

Group tutors and other staff who have a lot of contact with a particular pupil should make sure that they know:

- What the home circumstances are. Does the pupil live with parents, step-parents or with a foster parent? Who is the pupil's primary carer?
- Who has *parental responsibility* under The Children Act 1989? (See below.)
- Who has the right to see the pupil in school?
- Who is legally responsible for making decisions about the child's education?
- Who should be contacted in an emergency and where they can be found?
- Who should be sent copies of letters, reports, invitations, etc?

All these facts should be noted in the 'Pupil information' section in the pupil's files.

Parental responsibility is

Defined as 'all the rights, duties, powers, responsibilities and authority which by law a parent of a child has in relation to the child and his property' [S3(1)].

Parental responsibility can be exercised by persons who are not the child's biological parent and can be shared among a number of persons. It can be acquired by agreement or court order.

(Home Office, Department of Health, Department for Education and Employment, Welsh Office, 1991, p.123).

This means, for example, that, although the birth mother automatically has parental responsibility for her child, the father of a child does not automatically have parental responsibility unless, (a) he is married to the child's mother at the time of the child's birth, (b) he has been granted responsibility by the courts, or (c) the father has entered into a 'parental responsibility agreement' with the mother.

Areas for parental/carer involvement

The following links will be maintained.

Externally:
- follow-up school work at home
- help in setting and reviewing targets for achievement in learning
- help in setting and reviewing targets for achievement in behaviour
- fund-raising
- taking part in school functions
- donating materials/time
- parent governors.

Internally:
- help within the classroom (basic chores)
- help to support pupils with difficulties in basic skills
- listen to good readers
- give attention, praise and encouragement to certain pupils
- organize facilities for other parents
- drop into the school for a cup of coffee
- help with school functions
- help with school journeys.

Parents/carers are more likely to be effectively involved within the school if they:
- understand the way in which the school organizes the management of learning
- understand the way in which behaviour is managed
- know who is 'in charge' and who to refer to for help
- are given specific tasks .

Note: it should be made clear to any parents/carers who help in schools that they are there as helpers and not teachers. No amount of help or support in the classroom can make up for the skills of the professional teacher. They must clearly understand that they are there to assist the children to learn under the direction of the class teacher. The teaching unions have clear and useful advice on the use of helpers in classrooms.

Meetings with parents/carers

Often, teachers only meet parents/carers when there is something to be put right. If parents/carers do not feel at ease, or feel that they have been 'sent for', they will resent the meeting and are unlikely to cooperate with the school in this process.

The following guidelines will be followed, wherever practicable:

- parents will be told the reason for the meeting in advance
- the invitation will be in person (or over the telephone) and confirmed in writing. (Parents have been known to forget meetings!)
- invitations to the meeting will be couched in positive and welcoming terms
- the time of the meeting will fit in with the family's commitments
- the parent/carer will be invited to bring a friend, relative or social worker to the meeting with them
- there will be an interpreter present, if necessary
- other key members of the school community will be involved.
- all the information necessary for the meeting will be to hand
- the parents' room will be available for any other children who might be brought into the meeting and for making refreshments
- the greetings will friendly and informal, using names
- an interest will be expressed in the family as a whole
- it will be demonstrated that the child is valued
- the subject for discussion will be explained to the parents/carers and they will be asked if there is anything they want to raise during the meeting.
- it will be established what the school and the parents/carers want to achieve from the meeting
- the meeting will start with comments about the child in positive terms and in as non-judgmental a manner as possible
- the problem, if this is the subject of the meeting, will be explained in as positive a manner as possible
- the parents'/carers' opinions about possible solutions will be asked from time to time
- a check will be made from time to time that the parents'/carers' perception of what has been discussed matches the school's
- what has been decided will be summarized at the end and it will be checked that the parents/carers agree
- the parents/carers will be asked if there is anything else which needs to be covered
- the parents/carers and school will agree targets for further action, including a further meeting, if necessary.

In addition, where there is a dispute between parents/carers and the school over the handling of their child, an independent chair who is able to meet with the parents/carers before the meeting will be used.

In general, the school will try to ensure that parents/carers are:

- approached in a sensitive manner
- made to feel part of the process of defining the problem and seeking solutions
- made to feel at home in the school
- in agreement with and understand what has been decided.

After the meeting:

- a brief report will be written about what the issue was, what was agreed should be done and the targets for those involved
- it will be checked that the child agrees with it and it will be altered, if necessary
- a copy will be sent to the parents/carers for their comments and it will be altered in the light of these, if necessary.

Reporting to parents/carers

The school will provide regular reports to parents/carers about progress in learning and in behaviour. In general, reports to parents/carers will:

- concentrate on small target steps
- avoid general comments like, 'He's been good today'
- describe actual appropriate behaviour related to the pupil's targets: 'She has stayed in her seat all day'
- leave a space for the parents'/carers' own comments and so they can give examples of appropriate behaviour at home
- report daily
- be discussed with the child (and read to him or her, if necessary) before it is sent to the parents/carers.

Communications from parents/carers will be:

- made known to all appropriate staff
- filed carefully and referenced in the school's 'Day book'
- noted in the school's 'Day book'.

The *Good News!* card (see Figure 7.1, p.77) will be used to report to parents.

Appendix II Useful organizations

The Association of Workers for Children with Emotional and Behavioural Difficulties (AWC EBD)
Administrative Office: Allan Rimmer, AWC EBD, Charlton Court, East Sutton, Maidstone, Kent, ME17 3DQ; Tel: 01622 843104

The association exists to represent the interests of disturbed children and to promote communication between all the professional workers involved in working with them. It offers a range of regional and national events. *Emotional and Behavioural Difficulties* is published three times a year and is supplemented by publications on specific topics, including two newsletters a year.

Behaviour Matters
3 Woodlands Mews, Brigstock, Kettering, Northamptonshire NN14 3LX; Tel: 01536 373370

Behaviour Matters works with schools, parents and carers to:

- review, develop and implement whole-school behaviour policies;
- develop and implement behaviour management procedures in the classroom, around the school and with difficult pupils;
- counsel pupils whose learning and behaviour is being affected by emotional difficulties;
- counsel members of staff who are suffering from stress or trauma;
- help to set up support procedures for staff and direct support for senior staff;
- advise and train governors on all aspects of behaviour;
- advise on staff relationships;
- counsel and advise school staff following trauma;
- act as consultants to newly appointed heads and governors on behaviour policies;
- act as liaison between home and school where parents are concerned about the school's actions;
- review, develop and implement whole-school policies for child and staff protection;
- advise, counsel and train the designated teacher for child protection in line with the Children Act 1989;
- review, counsel and train on all aspects of bullying, pupil and staff;
- provide training on all aspects of self-esteem enhancement;
- advise on appropriate special provision for pupils with emotional and behavioural difficulties.

Childline
Freepost 1111, London N1 0BR; Tel: 0171 234 1000 (Hotline: 0800 1111)

Childline provides a free 24-hour telephone counselling service for children and young people.

Countering Bullying Unit (CBU)
Cardiff Institute of Higher Education, Cyncoed Road, Cardiff CF2 6XD; Tel: 0222 551111

Provides day conferences, training for schools staffs, advice and guidance, a resource base and advice on research.

Forum for the Advancement of Educational Therapy and Therapeutic Teaching (FAETT)
Honorary Secretary: Gerda Hanko, 3 Templewood, Ealing, London W13 8BA; Tel: 0181 998 4224

The forum aims to develop the theory of educational therapy, to encourage professional standards in its practice and to disseminate knowledge and understanding of the method.

It promotes the insights of teachers into emotional factors in learning and failure to learn and provides a forum for members to discuss their work and seek advice.

Kidscape
152 Buckingham Palace Road, London SW1W 9TR; Tel: 0171 730 3300

Kidscape aims to prevent abuse and bullying through education programmes involving teachers, other child care professionals and parents.

National Children's Bureau (NCB)
8 Wakley Street, London EC1V 7QE; Tel: 0171 843 6000

The NCB publishes a guide to training materials for teachers.

National Society for the Prevention of Cruelty to Children (NSPCC)
42 Curtain Road, London EC2A 3NH; Tel: 0171 825 2500

The NSPCC operates the National Child Protection Line (0800 800 500) offering counselling and advice for adults and children, and issues a series of publications on child protection.

Young Minds
22a Boston Place, London NW1 6ER; Tel: 0171 724 7262

Young Minds aims to:

- create greater national public awareness of the mental and emotional needs of children and young people and their families;
- ensure that public services in the health, social services, housing and voluntary sectors are well informed about the mental and emotional needs of children, young people and their families and carers, and conducive to the development of their mental health;
- promote the provision of a network of effective, accessible, multi-professional services for children and young people with mental and emotional problems, and their families.

When writing to these organizations for advice or information, please enclose an A5 size stamped, addressed envelope.

Appendix III Courses and training

The University of Birmingham
Certificate in Education, Diploma in Education, BPhil(Ed) or MEd
A modular, distance learning course in emotional and behavioural difficulties. It is designed for all those who work with children and young people with emotional and behavioural difficulties in mainstream, residential and day special schools and units
 Application forms from: The Admissions Office, School of Education, The University of Birmingham, Birmingham B15 2TT; Tel: 0121 414 4887.
 Informal enquiries to: John Visser (Course Tutor); Tel: 0121 414 3603.

Association of Workers for Children with Emotional and Behavioural Difficulties (AWC EBD) in association with Christchurch College, Canterbury
Certificate and Advanced Certificate (EBD); Counselling Skills Course
A modular course leading to a certificate and advanced certificate or as part of an advanced diploma in education. The course is designed to place emphasis on the relationship for individual workers between policy and practice.
 Further details from: AWC EBD, Carlton Court, East Sutton, Maidstone ME17 3DQ.
 Informal enquiries to: Allan Rimmer; Tel: 01622 843104.

Forum for the Advancement of Educational Therapy and Therapeutic Teaching (FAETT) in association with the Roehampton Institute
Aspects of Educational Therapy (An Introduction to Educational Therapy) and Diploma in Educational Therapy
The course is aimed at teachers and educational psychologists working in a variety of educational settings 'with specific areas of learning failure'.
 Further details from: FAETT, Alfington House, Church Lane, Alfington, East Devon EX11 1PE.
 Informal enquiries to: Heather Geddes; Tel: 01404 850329.

Lucky Duck Enterprises (Barbara Maines and George Robinson)
Workshops and training in the management of behaviour and bullying to schools throughout the country.
 Enquiries to: 10 Redland Terrace, Redland, Bristol BS6 6TG. Tel: 0117 9732881

References and Further Reading

Association of Metropolitan Authorities (1995) *Reviewing Special Educational Needs*, London: AMA.

Axline, V (1966) *Dibs in Search of Self*, London: Penguin.

Barker-Lunn, J (1984) 'Junior school teachers; their methods and practices', *Education Research*, 26, 3, 178–88.

Beane, J and Lipka, R (1984) *Self-concept, Self-esteem and the Curriculum*, Boston: Allyn and Bacon.

Cooper, P, Upton, G and Smith, C (1991) 'Ethnic minority and gender distribution among staff and pupils in facilities for pupils with emotional and behavioural difficulties in England and Wales', *British Journal of Sociology of Education*, 12, 1, 77–94.

Cooper, P, Smith, C and Upton, G (1994) *Emotional and Behavioural Difficulties: Theory to practice*, London: Routledge.

Coopersmith, S (1967) *The Antecedents of Self-esteem*, San Francisco, CA: Freeman.

Coopersmith, S and Feldman, R (1974) 'Fostering a positive self-concept and high self-esteem in the classroom', in Coop, R H and White, K (eds) *Psychological Concepts in the Classroom*, New York: Harper and Row.

Department of Education and Science (DES) (1989a) *Discipline in Schools* (The Elton Report), London: HMSO.

DES (1989b) *The Curriculum from 5–16* (2nd edn), London: HMSO.

DES (1989c) *School Teacher Appraisal: Report of the National Steering Group on the School Teacher Appraisal Pilot Study*, London: HMSO.

DES (1991) *Circular 12/91: School Teacher Appraisal*, London: HMSO.

Department for Education (DfE) (1993a) *National Exclusions Reporting System; Report on school exclusions*, London: HMSO.

DfE (1993b) *Circular 9/93: Protection of Children: Disclosure of criminal background of those with access to children*, London: HMSO.

DfE (1994a) *Bullying: Don't suffer in silence*, London: HMSO.

DfE (1994b) *Code of Practice on the Identification and Assessment of Special Educational Needs*, London: HMSO.

DfE (1994c) *Circular 9/94: The Education of Children with Emotional and Behavioural Difficulties*, London: DfE.

DfE (1994d) *Circular 8/94: Pupil Behaviour and Discipline*, London: DfE.

DfE (1995) *The National Curriculum*, London: HMSO.

Department for Education and Employment (DfEE) (1995a) *Circular 10/95: Protecting Children from Abuse: The role of the education service*, London: DfEE.

DfEE (1995b) *Circular 11/95: Misconduct of Teachers and Workers with Children and Young Persons*, London: DfEE.

Easen, P (1985) *Making School-centred INSET Work: A school of education pack for teachers*, Beckenham: Croom Helm.

Erikson, E (1968) *Identity, Youth and Crisis*, New York: WW Norton.

151

Grimshaw, R (1994) *Educating Disruptive Children*, London: National Children's Bureau.

Hamachek, D (1978) *Encounters with the Self* (2nd edn), New York: Holt, Rinehart and Winston.

Hargreaves, D, Hester, S and Mellor, F (1975) *Deviance in Classrooms*, London: Routledge and Kegan Paul.

HMSO (1988) *The Education Reform Act 1988*, London: HMSO.

HMSO (1989) *The Children Act 1989*, London: HMSO.

HMSO (1992) *The Education (Schools) Act 1992*, London: HMSO.

HMSO (1993) *The Education Act 1993*, London: HMSO.

Home Office, Department of Health, DfEE, Welsh Office (1991) *Working Together under The Children Act 1989*, London: HMSO.

Laslett, R and Smith, C (1993) *Effective Classroom Management* (2nd edn), London: Routledge.

Lawrence, D (1973) *Improved Reading and Counselling*, London: Ward Lock.

Lawrence, D (1987) *Improving Self-esteem in the Classroom*, London: Paul Chapman.

Lund, R (1987) 'The self-esteem of children with emotional and behavioural difficulties', *Maladjustment and Therapeutic Education*, 8, 2, 74–82.

Maines, B and Robinson, G (1992) *Bullying: The no-blame approach*, Bristol: Lucky Duck Publications.

Masson, J and Morris, M (1992) *Children Act Manual*, London: Sweet Maxwell..

Mortimore, P, Sammons, P, Stoll, L, Lewis, D and Ecob, R (1988) *School Matters: The junior years*, London: Open Books.

National Curriculum Council (NCC) (1989) *A Curriculum for All*, York: NCC.

NCC (1991) *Science and Pupils with Special Educational Needs*, York: NCC.

NCC (1993) *Science and Pupils with Special Educational Needs: A Workshop for Key Stages 1 and 2*, York: NCC.

Office for Standards in Education (OFSTED) (1993) *Education for Disaffected Pupils*, London: HMSO.

OFSTED (1995a) *Guidance on the Inspection of Nursery and Primary Schools*, London: HMSO.

OFSTED (1995b) *Guidance on the Inspection of Secondary Schools*, London: HMSO.

OFSTED (1995c) *Guidance on the Inspection of Special Schools*, London: HMSO.

OFSTED (1995d) *Framework for the Inspection of Schools*, London: HMSO.

Purkey, W and Novak, J (1984) *Inviting School Success: A self-concept approach to teaching and learning* (2nd edn), Belmont, CA: Wadsworth.

Pyke, N (1992) 'Warning in rise in exclusions', *Times Educational Supplement*, 17 April.

Pyke, N (1993) 'Banished to the exclusion zone', *Times Educational Supplement*, 26 April.

Rogers, C (1967) *On Becoming a Person: A therapist's view of psychotherapy* (2nd edn), London: Constable.

Rogers, C (1969) *Freedom to Learn*, Columbus, OH: Merrill.

Sammons, P, Hillman, J and Mortimore, P (1995) *Key Characteristics of Effective Schools: A review of school effectiveness research*, London: OFSTED.

Scheuer, A (1971) 'The relationship between personal attributes and effectiveness of teachers of emotionally disturbed children', *Exceptional Children*, 37, 723–31.

Schön, D (1983) *The Reflective Practitioner: How professionals think in action*, London: Temple Smith.

Smith, C and Laslett, R (1993) *Effective Classroom Control*, London: Routledge.

Stirling, M (1992) 'Squeezed out of a Combative World', *Times Educational Supplement*, 26 June.

Visser, J (1993) *Differentiation: Making it work*, Tamworth: NASEN Enterprises.

Wheldall, K and Merrett, F (1988) 'Discipline: rewarding work', *Teachers' Weekly*, 16 May, 25–7.

Wilson, M (1985) 'Teaching as therapy', *The Journal of Educational Therapy*, 1, 1, 75–87.

Other useful publications

Bliss, T and Tetley, J (1995) *Circle Time*, Bristol: Lucky Duck Publications.

Elliott, M (1989) *Responding to Child Abuse: The Kidscape training guide*, London: Kidscape.

Elliott, M (1991) *Bullying: A practical guide to coping for schools*, Harlow: Longman.

Faber, A and Mazlish, E (1980) *How to Talk so Kids will Listen and Listen so Kids will Talk*, New York: Avon Books.

Hanko, G (1995) *Special Needs in Ordinary Classrooms: From staff support to staff development* (3rd edn) London: David Fulton.

Herbert, C (1992) *Sexual Harassment in Schools: A guide for teachers*, London: David Fulton.

Kyriacou, C (1986) *Effective Teaching in Schools*, Oxford: Blackwell.

Maines, B and Robinson, G (1995) *You CAN… You KNOW you Can* (15th edn), Bristol: Lucky Duck Publications.

Maines, B and Robinson, G (1995) *Teacher Talk*, Bristol: Lucky Duck Publications.

Mongon, D and Hart, S (1989) *Improving Classroom Behaviour: New directions for teachers and pupils*, London: Cassell.

Moseley, J (1993) *Turn Your School Round*, Cambridge: LDA.

Robertson, J (1989) *Effective Classroom Control* (2nd edn), London: Hodder and Stoughton.

Robinson, G and Maines, B (1988) *They Can Because… A workshop in print*, Maidstone: AWC EBD.

Salzberger-Wittenberg, I, Henry, H and Osborne, E (1983) *The Emotional Experience of Teaching and Learning*, London: Routledge and Kegan Paul.

Tattum, D and Herbert, G (1990) *Bullying: A positive response*, Cardiff: Cardiff Institute of Higher Education.

Westmacott, E and Cameron, R (1981) *Behaviour can Change*, Basingstoke: Macmillan Education.

Young Minds (1995) *Violence and Young Minds: The effects of violence on children's mental health: Why bullying matters*, London: Young Minds.

Index